FINANCIALLY SPEAKING

THE BEST IMPROVEMENT STARTS WITH SELF IMPROVEMENT

Second Edition

MICHAEL "BART" MATHEWS

THE
MATHEWS
ENTREPRENEUR
GROUP, INC.

FINANCIALLY SPEAKING

THE BEST IMPROVEMENT STARTS WITH SELF IMPROVEMENT

Second Edition

CREATE YOUR OWN ECONOMIC STIMULUS PLAN

LET ME SHOW YOU HOW
Stop Living Pay Check to Pay Check
Don't Allow your Expenses to Exceed your Income
Improve your Financial Wealth by Changing your Thinking
Improve your Physical Health and Enjoy your Wealth
Create a Financial Legacy to pass on to your Children
Discover your power within, find your Secret to Success!

MICHAEL "BART" MATHEWS

THE
MATHEWS
ENTREPRENEUR
GROUP, INC.

Order this book online at www.trafford.com
or email orders@trafford.com
or www.tmeginc.com email: info@tmeginc.com

Most Trafford titles are also available at major online book retailers.

Cover image: "seamuss/Shuttershock.com"
Editor and Contributor - Robbie S Mathews, President, The Mathews Entrepreneur Group, Inc.

Print information available on the last page.

ISBN: 978-1-4251-4018-2 (sc)
ISBN: 978-1-4907-1867-5 (e)

Trafford rev. 09/22/2018

 www.trafford.com

North America & international
toll-free: 1 888 232 4444 (USA & Canada)
fax: 812 355 4082

PRAISE FOR FINANCIALLY SPEAKING

"Always interested in learning how to improve my situation, I eagerly read Michael Mathews' book, <u>Financially Speaking</u>, and was impressed by what I read. Speaking from his heart and personal experience, Michael speaks about how to get your finances in order. Since financial issues frequently are at the bottom of interpersonal issues in a marriage and stress-related health issues in a body, control over finances can be at the heart of improving these aspects of life as well.

The book is beautifully organized to cover the many aspects of financial life, starting from the negative side of the balance sheet by discussing steps to take to get out of debt, moving through managing money on a daily basis, and continuing on to preparing for the future by investing, insuring to cover unforeseen events, and teaching your children. Michael offers specifics, and references to places to get help or more information. He gives clear descriptions of the reasons for different considerations, and even includes a "dictionary" of terms.

<u>Financially Speaking</u> is a good read whether you're a novice at tackling managing your money or you're experienced. There are some good reminders and ideas which might not yet have come to mind. And all of it is presented with a sense

of joy, and personal touch, shown in the poems and anecdotes included to illustrate various points.

Michael Mathews is a person of caring and integrity, with a desire to help others improve their lives. I highly recommend "Financially Speaking."

-Carolyn R. Chase, Salt Lake City Utah
Masters of Arts-Teaching, Harvard University

"The book is a good resource for 18 and up to understand the value of money and how to make money work for you. The first chapter laid a foundation for me to understand the intricate details of money, learn from others mistakes and not to fall into those traps. The language used in the book is relatable and I can tell a person from a generation or two before me wrote the book due to the examples and sayings used, which offered another perspective into a culture that I appreciate."

-Bianca Spratt, Graduate Student, Chicago Illinois
Masters of Art in Applied Professional Studies

"The second edition of Financially Speaking: The Best Improvement Starts With Self Improvement is a guide to getting one's financial life back with step by step action plans. This book is a must-read for anyone who wants to get ahead financially, regardless of their present financial state. I recommend this book for anyone who wants to commit to self-improvement as a way of life. In addition to providing great tips on saving and growing your money, the author shares his wisdom for living life to its fullest! I commend author Michael "Bart" Mathews, on this brilliant literary work."

-Zed Braden, Attorney
Ainsworth & Associates PC, Chicago Illinois

"This document is a cure for sore eyes and the financially distressed. You have a plan for financial success if implemented with fidelity. This book has provided me with information that will benefit me and my offspring for generations. The book is elaborate but reader friendly."

-Leavelle Abram, Principal
Leaf Erickson School, Chicago Illinois

"Congratulations on another good one! Although it's been over 8 years (if not more), since I edited your first book, it was like a refresher in some ways; but also good and fresh information, for the most part. The chapters 5 thru 10 certainly increased my knowledge and were also "food for thought". I particularly gained lots of insight from the content in Chapters:

- 7 – Estate Planning

- 8 – The Deadly Killers – very educational and so real to our culture

- 9 – The Children really resonated with me because this is something we did not get as children, but it's such a blessing to pass it on to the youth in our families.

- 10 – Self Improvement – this resonates with me because self-improvement is continuous. Your tools and tips really add to the process of the overall self-improvement journey

Your poems are really awesome! Definitely something you should consider in the near future. Overall, I really enjoyed it. My biggest personal takeaway is to not be anxious to get the new car and purchase a condo, townhouse, etc., again until my finances say yes, without question. In summary, this is really good information and I'm sure the Lord will bless you exceedingly and abundantly because of your works – this book, which will help so many others!"

-Cathy Flowers-Oak Park, Illinois
Corporate Trainer/Fortune 500 Company

"Financially Speaking" is a blueprint for your financial success. It tells you how to get out of debt and pay yourself. It also shows you smart ways to invest and to build wealth for the rest of your life!"
-Dan Duster, Motivational Speaker/Professional Success Coach
Owner, 3D Development Group, Chicago, Illinois
Author: Peaceful Selling-Easy Sales Techniques to Grow Your Small Business

"Extremely well done, easy to follow, and covers a wide range of topics, which are intertwined to provide an overall strategic improvement for anyone seeking to "Live Long and Prosper." Michael Mathews, you provide a step by step, simple plan, which if followed as laid out, will help ensure a healthy, financial and successful path for virtually anyone."
-Mike Woods, Real Estate Agent and Investor
Century 21 Affiliated, Homewood, Illinois

"Michael thanks for your transparency on prevalent issues that plague our society. There's a great need for the wisdom and expertise depicted on these pages. You not only identify the pitfalls and their woes, but you also gave credible footage by providing the necessary tools to get you out and stay out of indebtedness. I also recommend this excellent read for young adults while transitioning into adulthood. Michael, you've been equipped for such an awesome task, keep arming the generations to come."
-La Sandra Gayle Thomas, President/Owner
Executive Producer/Writer/Film Maker
Sweet Pea Productions, NC Inc.
Greensboro, North Carolina

"Growing up, financial literacy was not a topic at the dinner table, although we boasted about what we wanted to be when we grow up and how much money we wanted to make. The lack of financial knowledge growing up in my early twenties contributed to a fear of finances altogether. Being a business owner, facing my fear of financial literacy became detrimental to my business. Mr. Mathew's book is very well done. Before I started reading it, I thought the content was going to be complicated because of my lack of enthusiasm. As soon as I started reading it, I became more enthusiastic about the potential of this book. The book is clear and concise and offers much more information than I expected in regards to the importance of financial literacy. Financially Speaking delivers an engaging interpretation and perspective on financial literacy. This book is an excellent resource for students, educators, and financial enthusiasts. In reviewing this book, the principal criteria included content, organization, and reference sources. Starting with the basic information of financial literacy such as; debt, expenses, credit history, the list goes on. It took me on a journey through the world of finances in which I had very little knowledge of. The tone of the book reflects a learned appreciation for understanding the power of managing your finances. And the best part, it includes poems that express the creativity of the author."

-Aini (Nura) Abukar
Entrepreneur, Chicago, Illinois

SPECIAL THANKS

A VERY SPECIAL THANK you goes to my wife, Robbie. You have supported all of my goals and dreams without hesitation. You believe that teamwork makes the dream work, and we make a great team. Your wisdom, knowledge, skills and life experiences have proved to be invaluable. Your forty-year professional career in corporate America has allowed you to exponentially grow by leaps and bounds.

Your all hands on deck team approach for the accomplishment of this project has always been your driving motivation for personal, family, and professional success.

With each written goal that we accomplish, we are one step closer to obtaining our dreams. Our vision is clear and concise. I love you and thank you for your unwavering support. May we continue down the path of our journey to and transform your Financial DNA For Life. May our overwhelming desire to serve others, while we serve ourselves, remain the cornerstone of our wealth building legacy.

To my 92-years-young mother, Clora, who remembers many of my failures and never lost faith that I would be successful! I love you.

"Money isn`t the most important thing in life, but it`s reasonably close to oxygen on the gotta have it scale!"

-Zig Ziglar

TABLE OF CONTENTS

ACKNOWLEDGEMENTS

Leavelle Abram
Aini (Nura) Abukar
Nakii Rapheal Barnes
Zedrick Braden
Caroline Chase
Dr. James "JD" Dentley
Dan Duster
Cathy Flowers
Dr. Kara Scott Dentley
Janina Marie Spencer
Bianca Spratt
LaSanda Gayle Thomas
Nadia Sky Tucker
Nathalia Starr Tucker
Sandy Whetstone
Mike Woods

I WANT TO EXPRESS my heartfelt gratitude to each and every one of you for your unwavering support. I really appreciate every individual comment, suggestion, and written statement. The many words of wisdom and encouragement helped me overcome several adversities, turning them into seeds of greatness. The results of your due diligence helped me, an ordinary man, to complete this extraordinary accomplishment. I hope I have met your high level of standard of excellence, as you have far exceeded all of my expectations in return. My riches do not lie in material wealth, it comes from having family and friends like you! Because of our teamwork, we made this dream work. I flew higher than an eagle because you were the wind beneath my wings! I want to thank you all for sharing your light, from the universe, with me on this journey!

                                              -Michael Bart Mathews

PREFACE

THIS BOOK WAS written because of our commitment to spread financial literacy education on a global scale to the masses. We believe that Financially Speaking - The Best Improvement Starts With Self Improvement. From our many conversations with ordinary people; who were looking for an extraordinary financial read; this book is for you. There are also nuggets for you corporate climbers, business owners and entrepreneurs.

No matter what country you live in, what currency you use, or what language you speak; the bottom line on a global scale is; improving one's financial literacy education is on the forefront of economic development, growth, and transformation.

Because of our desire to share our 7 LIVE W.E.A.L.T.H.Y. PRINCIPLES, we have had the privilege to speak Internationally in several countries and domestically in the United States on the importance of financial literacy education.

In February of 2017, we launched our 7 LIVE W.E.A.L.T.H.Y. PRINCIPLES in the beautiful country of South Africa in front of 1,200 plus attendees from 21 countries while in Johannesburg. We also spoke directly to the South African people through the media which consisted of articles in the Saturday Star and the Sunday Times newspapers, KAYA/FM 98 and 93.8FM Mix radio interviews, and a live ANN7 BIZPULSE Business News television appearance.

During a trip to Cannes, France we had the opportunity to do a live radio interview on FM Radio France.

In November 2017, we shared our 7 LIVE W.E.A.L.T.H.Y. PRINCIPLES on stage in front of 2,500 attendees from 71 different countries in Los Angeles, California.

We have been featured in the following magazines The Global Man & The Global Woman (London), Business Woman Today (London), WORKLIFE (Australia), Business Booster Today (Germany). We have also been featured on CAN TV and 102.3FM WYCA/Rejoice Radio in the Chicagoland area. Our message has been featured globally throughout different media outlets; and we are just getting started!

I interviewed NFL Chicago Bear-1985 Super Bowl Championship Coach-Mike Ditka in Chicago and actor Al Pacino (The Godfather) in Los Angeles. My wife, Robbie, interviewed Ndaba Mandela (Nelson Mandela's grandson) in South Africa. All three men shared their unanimous support for the importance of financial literacy education from their personal financial transformational perspectives.

Les Brown, one of the world's renowned motivational speakers, whom we've had the privilege of sharing the stage with says, "You don't have to be great to get started, but you have to get started to be great."

In order for you to get started, your first critical decision is to keep turning the pages of this book. You cannot keep on doing the same thing and expect a different financial outcome! We all know that is the definition of insanity. Your second critical decision is to change how you think about your money. Your third critical decision-you must change how you feel about money. And, your fourth critical decision-you must change how you act (spend) with your money!

Now turn the page and read on to discover how becoming financially educated and empowered can transform your Financial DNA For Life.

INTRODUCTION

*"If anyone's gonna write about me. I reckon it
be me/myself."*

-Langston Hughes

I PUBLISHED THE FIRST edition of this book in 2008 because
I believed that some of my past financial adversities have
been experienced to some degree by hundreds, thousands
and maybe millions of everyday people all across the globe.
I wanted to share with you how I changed a life of financial
disparity by finding my seeds of economic greatness through
financial literacy education.

However, in 2008, the nation experienced a severe
economic collapse. Millions of people across all six living
generations faced situations such as the Wall Street meltdown,
bursting of the housing bubble and health care issues, just to
name a few. This contributed to corporate downsizing, loss
of employment, loss of income, loss of lifestyle and in some
cases, divorce and loss of life.

Many people who were affected had to deplete their life
savings (if they had any) trying to keep their heads above
water. They drew down 401k plans, IRAs and suffered early
withdrawal penalties because some were under the age of 59

½. They sunk deeper into credit card debt trying to keep food on the table. No longer able to pay the mortgage, rent, car note and credit card payments, bankruptcy filings skyrocketed. Across the country, car repossessions soared; foreclosure and short sales proceedings were widespread, tenants evictions were rampant, all resulting in an increase in homelessness. You name it, it happened.

Now in 2015, it appears that the global economy is trying to rebound. Financial literacy and preparedness are at the forefront of conversations in homes, coffee shops, barber shops, gyms, newspapers, television, radio and other media outlets everywhere. Therefore, I decided to write this second edition of Financially Speaking to again share with you key financial principles that changed my life in many tremendous ways.

My goal is to motivate, encourage, stimulate and inspire you to take a deep, honest look at your total overall present day financial situation. My hope is that you will discover what changes you can make, then take action and make those changes! You have the ability to create your own Economic Stimulus Plan while increasing your understanding and knowledge of financial literacy and wealth-building principles.

Most importantly, I really want to emphasize the need for teaching financial literacy in every household and school in every community throughout the United States and beyond. Teaching children at a young age the basic building blocks of financial literacy is the cornerstone for helping to change a family's economic dynamics for generations to come. Just like material possessions are passed down, why not pass down financial literacy knowledge and education!

This book has the same key financial principles, core values and concepts from the first edition along with updated statistics and information valuable to the various generations living today. The media, marketers and various other organizations (Census Bureau, Harvard Center, etc.) have varied opinions as to the start and end date ranges for each of the generational groups. In 2015, the generations listed below fall somewhere within the indicated date ranges by year and age:

- GI/Greatest and Silent Generations - born between 1901 and 1945 (age 114 to 70) –You are most likely receiving a company pension and/or social security benefits. Medicare, Medicaid, and other social programs may be required to help provide a decent, sustainable standard of living.
- Baby Boomers – born between 1946 and 1964 (age 69 to 51) - I am in this group. We have the least amount of time remaining to grow a retirement nest egg. Some of us have saved and prepared for retirement, some have not. Some are receiving the same benefits as the Silent generation.
- Generation X – born between 1965 and 1980 (age 50 to 35) – You still have time to learn financial literacy, create an economic stimulus plan and aggressively build and manage your retirement nest egg.
- Millennials/Generation Y- born between 1981 and 2000 (age 16 to 36) – I'm speaking directly to you. 2015 is an opportune time (the economy is rebounding) for you to begin to take financial literacy education and planning seriously. If you have not already done so, create your economic stimulus plan. This book is a must read for you!
- Generation Z/Boomlets – born in 2000 (age 15) – the children are our future. This group is social, visual, technological and impressionable. You will have significant influence and impact on the economy in the next 10 years and beyond. Parents now is the time for you to teach your children about financial literacy education. Help children learn financial principals as soon as possible!

———

Before I get into the meat of this book, let me share with you some of my past, early in life, self-inflicted financial mistakes that literally caused my downfall. As you read my story, pay close attention to where you are today. More importantly, where you want to be in five, ten, fifteen or twenty years from now, Financially Speaking of course! In my younger years, I did not take personal responsibility for my cash flow and practiced awful spending habits. So, I suffered the consequences of my financially destructive actions from the choices I made.

My debt and spending got completely out of control even though I was always gainfully employed, with enough positive cash flow to pay my way. One of the financial keys that I failed to follow early on was to understand the importance of balancing my checkbook. I did not log all withdrawals, deposits, interest or fees. Instead, I kept a guesstimate of what I thought my balance was and I paid a significant amount in overdraft fees as a result.

I could no longer stay current with my car payments and received late and overdue notices from the bank. After awhile I stopped opening the mail. Eventually, late payments became the norm, then soon after, I made no payments at all. My car was repossessed, my credit cards were maxed out. The credit card companies tried to work with me by reducing the monthly payment amount. I still did not pay because by now it was clear to me that my expenses had exceeded my income, and my upkeep became my downfall. I accumulated other unpaid bills and neglected them as well.

I could barely hold my head above water and was sinking fast. I was drowning in the sea of debt looking for a financial life preserver to save me from myself! I finally had to file for bankruptcy.

What I learned from those early years in life was, through every adversity there was a seed of greatness. My adversity stemmed from my need for immediate gratification, the lack of practicing personal financial literacy principals, filing for bankruptcy, car repossession, and bad credit. My declining credit score and depleted savings were other contributing factors. I looked in the mirror at myself and I did not like the man who was staring back at me. My personal self-esteem hit an all-time low and I experienced a moment of emotional bankruptcy. I spent years enrolled in the "University of Hard Knocks" because of my personal financial literacy shortcomings. I needed to find the seed of greatness within me.

Have you ever heard the phrase, "Don't cry over spilled milk?" Well, I did not cry over my adversity. Instead, I did something about it. I changed my thinking and took personal responsibility for my failures. I formulated and wrote down on paper a set of short-term, mid-range and long-term goals followed by a plan of action that would lead me down the path of personal financial success. All I had to do was stay focused, stay positive, and stay the course. I re-read my goals morning, noon and night, day in and day out!

Making the decision to change my past financial adversities was like a breath of fresh air for my soul and my self-esteem. I knew what I just went through was a low point in my life, but that did not matter. What did matter was where I was going for the remainder of my life.

There was no room for error at this point. For me to change my financial status, I had to continue to change my thinking and become more financially literate. I never took the time to understand words like portfolio, stocks trading on the New York Stock Exchange, Nasdaq and the S&P 500, bull or bear market, bonds, and mutual funds, private equity investments.

I didn't understand what taxes were, let alone paying them, and to whom and why. What happens if you don't pay your taxes? And who was good old Uncle Sam? I knew I didn't have an Uncle named Sam. But I found out the hard way that Uncle Sam was the State and Federal Government Tax Authorities!

Once I decided to start my plan of action, my financial literacy knowledge and my life quickly began to improve. I started listening to tapes concerning business and personal financial matters while driving instead of listening to music on the radio. I also started reading financial books and magazines. I applied for a library card and it opened the door to a ton of resource material that I could read and borrow for free. I had no more excuses for not learning about financial literacy principles and concepts. I was no longer standing in my way. I was transforming and starting to think, act and feel more positive about money.

With time and patience, I was able to re-establish my credit. I started rebuilding my credit by opening up a couple of credit accounts and paying them on time or early. Next, I opened a new checking and savings account and started paying myself first.

Another significant change in my life happened when I began to associate with like-minded positive-thinking people who readily shared their financial expertise, knowledge, wisdom and experience with me which further enhanced my financial literacy self-improvement journey.

I went from being in debt, with no money left over at the end of the month, to paying off considerable amounts of debt in record time using my debt reduction rollover payment plan. Next the education of investing versus savings for the long-term took center stage. In other words, a real introduction to building wealth was nurtured.

I was blessed to marry a wonderful woman, Robbie, with whom I was able to put all my cards on the table and share my past financial misfortunes with. Together we made a joint plan of action to ensure success for our future. We both joined the "Blessed to Invest" investment club that stressed financial literacy education, which taught us both about more investments options. This allowed us to start looking into investment opportunities outside of our employer-sponsored investment programs.

As my financial literacy increased (as yours can too), I was mindful not to repeat any of my past financial blunders. As a result, my newfound knowledge helped me overcome many obstacles. If I had not changed the short-sighted way I was thinking, feeling and misusing my money, I honestly do not know what situation I would be in today. I finally graduated from a life full of economic adversity by finding my financial seed of greatness through financial literacy education, because "The Best Improvement Starts with Self-Improvement."

I am very passionate and concerned about the 80 million plus Millennials-Gen Y. You still have time on your side to pull yourself up by your bootstraps and make right any financial wrongs that you might be experiencing. I am sure you have heard others discuss financial planning, retirement, and wealth-building principles sometime in your everyday walk of life.

You may have taken some economic courses in high school or college. Do you remember what you learned? Did you ever use those economic principles for financial self-improvement? You now have the opportunity to begin your real personal financial literacy education journey regardless of your current financial status!

You might be saying to yourself, I'm young, that financial planning stuff doesn't apply to me, that's for rich people with large estates. You might be thinking that retirement is like speaking a foreign language or it may not have crossed your mind because of your age! You might also be thinking that you have plenty of time to take care of your golden years, right? Well, I thought the very same thing when I was your age.

Boy, Oh Boy was I wrong! I didn't realize that retirement was not about age. It is about money! I totally disregarded another financial key, the "pay yourself first at least 10% of all you earn" rule, and yes it cost me hundreds of thousands of dollars over time. Financially Speaking, being a wandering generality (no plan) instead of a meaningful specific (have a plan) with your personal finances can be costly!

If you are in the Millennial/Generation Y age group (18 to 34) you should START TODAY, not tomorrow, not next week, not next month, not next year. You will have more time to get out of debt, build an emergency fund, grow your retirement nest egg and create wealth. While not leaving thousands, in some cases hundreds of thousands, in others cases even millions of dollars on the table. By planning your financial future NOW, you will develop a peace of mind knowing that the next 30+ years of actively managing a well thought out financial action plan for success is in place. You will no longer be a wondering generality! The time to take responsibility is NOW!

———

There are financial keys to success for everyone who is searching for a better, happier, and more satisfying lifestyle, regardless of your current age. You cannot put a price tag on intelligence because intelligence is priceless. But ignorance will cost you dearly!

You cannot worry and stress yourself out about your past financial roadblocks or those experienced by others. The past is the past, get over it and act in the present so you will have a bright, prosperous future. There is nothing shameful when things in your life don't go as planned. The only shame would be to allow negative people and negative situations to hold you back. The only person that can hold you back is that person you see when you look in the mirror. Stop for a moment and think, are you going to let that person help you or defeat you? You have complete control over what you will and will not do in life because of how you think. The choice is yours; if you fail to plan, you plan to fail! Any excuse can be used as a reason to fail. If you think you can, you can. If you think you can`t, you can`t, either way you`re right.

This entire book offers a chance for you to look at several different financial success keys that can help lead to future success. You first must change how you think, act and feel about money, accept your shortcomings, be willing to self-educate and finally spring into action allowing a change from past practice.

I do have personal experience in all of these areas. I am not ashamed to say that I failed my way to success. Had I not taken financial literacy education and self-improvement seriously; you might not be reading this book. Maybe you or somebody you know might have shared similar experiences.

We all make mistakes or have unforeseen circumstances enter into our lives; just don't keep on making the same mistakes or letting your past define your present or future financial accomplishments. You have the ability to change some things in your life just as I did.

It's not what side of the tracks you come from, or what you have done in the past that count. It's where you are right now, today and where you want to be in the future that count. It's not who you are or what you are that count. It's who and what you want to become that matters!

This book is for all people who can use some inspiration and motivation while getting or staying on the right financial track. Regardless if you graduated from high school or obtained your GED. It doesn't matter if you were a college dropout (some of the wealthiest millionaires and billionaires in the world were college dropouts) or hold a Master's or Ph.D. The individual, self-motivated innovator who acquires financial literacy education can help level the economic playing field for all who seek her wisdom.

Please don't misunderstand the above paragraph, a brick and mortar institutionalized formal education being taught by the most talented, trained minds in the world is second to none. I support education to the fullest! And by having a plan for success, taking action to make it happen and surrounding yourself with great financial minds and advisors, you can succeed in spite of anything if you want success bad enough!

Financially successful people are not people without problems. Everyone experience problems! Successful people are people who have learned how to solve their problems by using the knowledge they acquired themselves and from others. They see problems or obstacles as opportunities for positive change.

I hope my personal experiences gives you some valuable insights. As you begin your financial literacy educational journey, start associating with successful people who are currently where you want to be. Accept personal responsibility for your actions and remember, "You Can Do It." Review your current situation. Look at all the events that led you to where you are today. Your past life experiences along with your dedication to financial literacy education will help you transfer from the "University of Hard Knocks" to the "University of Lifeology" to pursue your Ph.D. in "Financial Literacy Education"!

I invite you to read on and discover insights that should help you to take a more holistic view of your personal finances because any one of them has the ability to positively or negatively impact your overall financial bottom line.

Let me share with you some financial keys to success. Throughout this book, you will find financial literacy topics and definitions, such as; types of income, assets, liabilities (debt), banking, saving, investing, taxes, insurance, and health, that you should try to fully understand by the time you finish reading this book.

There are many helpful tips and eye openers that you can research and decide which ones are best for you. Regardless of age, if you are single, married, divorced, young just starting out, currently in college, or retired, this book can help prevent you from making some costly financial mistakes. I also wrote several poems that are placed throughout this book to help motivate, stimulate, and inspire you along the way.

At the end of the day, you and only you will decide what changes you need to make, then you must take action and self-educate yourself if you want to change your financial outlook.

The volume of information contained within may appear to be overwhelming but it is not hard. Simple math, an open mind, and common sense are all you need to start gaining an understanding of your personal finances. I suggest focusing on one chapter at a time and start making the necessary personal financial changes as you go along. Don't try to do everything all at once. Do not wait until you finish reading this book to get started! Chapter 2-Debt Management and Chapter 3-Credit Management are the largest and most important chapters to begin your journey. Be sure to really spend the necessary time to thoroughly read and understand these chapters. This next step continues you on your journey on how you can continue to transform your Financial DNA For Life.

REMEMBER, "THE BEST IMPROVEMENT STARTS WITH SELF-IMPROVEMENT."

POEM - THE BEST IMPROVEMENT STARTS WITH SELF IMPROVEMENT

When you look in the mirror, who do you see

Are you that person that you want to be

While going through life, do you think in your mind

I know I was made, just one of a kind

Yard by yard life can be hard

But inch by inch life is a cinch

Self-improvement may be hard to accept

You know in your heart, you should not reject

In your elder days will you look back and say

I gave life my all, until my very last day

Learn all you can while your mind is sharp

Because unused knowledge will one day depart

-MICHAEL "BART" MATHEWS

CHAPTER 1
DEBT MANAGEMENT

*"Don`t let your expenses exceed your income,
Or your upkeep will become your downfall."*

-MICHAEL *"BART"* MATHEWS

WHAT IS DEBT?

Any amount of money borrowed and owed by one party to another.

DEBT IS WHEN you borrow money from a source (bank for a home loan, credit card company, automobile loan, student loan, family member or friend) and have an unpaid balance.

Debt is the root of financial evil. It is very easy to accumulate debt, and it takes a long time to get that "gorilla" off your back. Especially, if you don`t have a debt reduction rollover payment plan in place. My debt was self-inflicted; I caused my own financial demise early in life.

As stated in the introduction, I was deep in debt. I let my expenses exceed my income, causing my upkeep to become my downfall. I did not realize how much debt I accumulated (reckless spending, no bookkeeping) until it was too late. All I did was charge, charge, charge. I had credit card debt and other revolving credit. You name it, I owed it. My financial ship started to sink until I said enough is enough. No more debt!

Unfortunately, due to the economic crisis that started in 2008, millions of people found themselves in debt that was beyond their control. Some lost their jobs. Their bank accounts were drained. Retirement plans and pensions were lost. Some lost their automobiles, lost homes to foreclosure or short sales, some couples even got divorced. As a result, many people unexpectedly found themselves having to go into debt just to survive. The impact of debt is the same regardless of how you accumulated it. If you do not or you cannot pay your bills, the outcome is the same.

Debt causes unwanted stress. Debt causes you to look at the caller ID on your telephone and when you see it is a bill collector, you let the call go to voicemail. If you do answer, you say "I am sorry (your name) isn't home, may I take a message?" Debt causes you to hide your vehicle, to avoid repossession, until you can catch up with the payments. If you are in a relationship filled with debt, it can cause disagreements with your spouse or partner, sometimes resulting in divorce or the demise of your relationship.

Debt is a silent and deadly killer of your financial present and future. Debt has a way of creeping up on you if you are not closely monitoring your spending (charging) habits. You probably began your debt destruction by using credit cards for almost everything from breakfast, lunch, and dinner. Are you buying things you do not need, with money you do not have (credit), to impress people you do not even know or like? This is called, "Keeping up with the Joneses" or for the younger generations; the reality TV stars, you know who they are!

In order to keep up with the Joneses, you start making bigger purchases. You buy your $50,000 dream car which depreciated in value as soon as you drove it off the lot. It came equipped with a big fat car note of $800.00 per month for 72 months (6 years) with an interest rate of 5% (depending upon your credit score). This results in a total of approximately

$58,000 in lengthy payments, not including taxes and other fees. To go along with the car, you dress it up with new tires, rims to match and a booming stereo sound system adding additional expense.

Now you must dress yourself up, so you buy the latest trendy designer fashions. Ladies, Jimmy Choo, Michael Kors, Coach, Gucci, and Prada, have all become your BFFs. Fellas you look like you stepped out of a GQ magazine in your Armani suits paired with your Adidas and Nike designer kicks. While you are looking good and smelling good, the inside of your purse or wallet has no cash, just plastic filled with debt and prolonged destruction.

Do not forget about all the other accessories, such as gold and diamond rings, tennis bracelets, furs, leather coats, and alligator or snakeskin shoes. Last, but not least, is your house, condo, or apartment filled with Ultra HD 4K LED flat screen wall mounted TVs in every room? Cable or satellite connections that get every channel you can think of without you having enough time to watch them. Do not forget the expensive furnishings that you never let anyone sit on or touch because you bought them just for show because you are trying to keep up with the Joneses.

The reason I mentioned the home last is because cars, clothes and jewelry appear to be more important to some people than actually buying a home. As a matter of fact, some of you are still living at home with your parents escaping the responsibilities of adulthood. You rack up on all the material items you can accumulate, instead of saving or investing early. Unfortunately, since you have no mortgage, rent or other major living expense responsibilities, you may not have any incentive to become financially responsible. Financial responsibility comes with being self-sufficient, disciplined and paying your own way.

However, many of you did do the responsible thing and bought homes and were living the American dream, until the bottom fell out of the housing market causing hundreds of thousands of homes to lose value. Unfortunately, the dream then turned into a nightmare called foreclosure because the value of the home dropped lower than the outstanding mortgage balance. That's called being under water or upside down in value! It was hard to sell and even harder to get your home refinanced. Now you are between a rock and a hard place.

Regardless if it was your dream home, dream car, luxuries or basic necessities that were purchased with Other People's Money (OPM), you now need to begin "managing" your debt. You need to understand the components of each of your credit cards and loans.

Let us look closer at what happens when you use OPM, better known as credit. Using credit is an expensive way of using tomorrow's money today. There is a big price in repayment costs for using OPM (credit) and that price is called interest and fees and debt!

HOW IS INTEREST CALCULATED?

How is interest calculated? There is a variety of different formulas used to calculate interest based on the type of loan or credit you are receiving and whether you are receiving interest. I will address 3 types; Simple Annual Accrued Interest, Annual Compound Interest, and Credit Card Interest.

Savings Simple Annual Interest

For interest earned on savings, the formula for Simple Annual Accrued Interest is:

$A = P(1 + rT)$. It may look a little complicated, but all you have to do is replace your savings numbers with the letters per the definitions below and do the math:

- P=Starting Principal Amount
- R=Annual Percentage Rate (APR) ; $r = R/100$ is APR converted to decimal
- T=Time Period for Savings - in months or years
- I=Interest Earned (total accrued amount – principal)
- A=Total Accrued Amount of Principal + Interest

For example, how much interest would you earn in 5 years on a $12,000 investment at an annual interest rate of 6.00%?

Formula version: $15,600(A) = $12,000(P) x (1 + (6.00/100=.06) (r) x 5 years(T)). This means you will earn $3,600 ($15,600 - $12,000) in interest.

If you are like me and are not a math formula wizard, I had to break it down into steps:

1. Convert Annual Percentage **(R)ate** into a decimal (6%/100) = **(r)ate** =.06
2. Multiply **(r)ate** by **(T)ime Period** (.06 x 5) = .30
3. Add 1.00 to the **Time Period Rate** = (1 + .30) = 1.30
4. Multiply the **(P)rincipal** by the rate from Step 3 ($12,000 x 1.30) = $15,600 **(A)ccrued Amount**
5. Determine **(I)nterest Earned** = ($15,600 - $12,000) = $3,600 is the answer

Savings Compound Annual Interest

The formula for Annual Compound Interest on savings is similar to Simple Annual Accrued Interest but a little more complex: $A = P(1 + rT)^{nt}$, where (n) is the number of times interest is compounded per year (e.g. n=12 for monthly compounding). I am listing the formula but won't break it down as I did above.

Basically, the concept of compound interest is that interest is added back to the principal sum so that interest is also earned on the added interest during the next compounding period. Interest can be compounded for any period of time, but daily, monthly, quarterly or annually are the most common periods used.

Using the same figures from above, if the interest was compounded annually for those 5 years, your interest earned would be $9,490 ($21,490 - $12,000) instead of $3,600. You can see how compounding can make your savings grow significantly.

Once you fully understand the formula for simple interest, search the internet for the formula for compound interest and give it a try using your savings values. There are many calculators available to help you with your calculations.

Credit Card Interest

The formula to calculate credit card interest is also a little more complex but straightforward. There are 4 parts to be calculated: Average Daily Balance, Periodic (Daily) Interest Rate, Periodic (Daily) Interest Charged and Total Period Interest Charge. For our example, we will calculate the interest due for a 31 day month (e.g. January):

1. Step 1 – calculate the **average daily balance**. For example, let's say that you have a $5,000 balance at the end of the January. You don't use your credit card at all during this month, but on the 16th day, you make a payment of $300. So, the balance for days 1-15 is $5,000, and the balance for days 16-31 is $4,700. Add up each of the **daily balances for the month**, and then divide that number by the **number of days in the month** to get your **average daily balance**:
    (15 x 5,000) + (16 x 4,700) = (75,000 + 75,200) / 31 = 4,845.16 is the **average daily balance**

2. Step 2 - calculate the **periodic interest rate**. If your **annual percentage rate** (APR) is 18% convert it to a decimal (18.00/100=0.18), then divide that by 365:
    (0.18/365) = 0.00049 is your **periodic (or daily) interest rate**

3. Step 3 – calculate the **periodic (daily) interest charge**. Multiply your periodic interest rate by your average daily balance:
    (4,845.16 x 0.00049) = 2.37 is the **periodic (daily) interest charge**

4. Calculate the **Total Interest Charged** for the period (month) - multiply the periodic (daily) interest charge by the **number of days in the month** to get the **interest charged**:
    (2.37 x 31) = $73.47 is your **Total Interest Charge** for January

Review your monthly credit statements. Find the annual percentage rate (APR) you are being charged, the original principal balance, the outstanding principal balance, and the monthly payment amount. The original principal balance is the original dollar amount borrowed. The outstanding principal is the amount remaining after the monthly payment is applied. Look at how much of your monthly payment is actually paying down the original principal balance and how much is going towards interest. Initially, the majority of your monthly payment goes towards interest which is why you stay in debt so long.

Let's assume in this example your minimum monthly payment on a $5,000 credit card balance is $110.00. If you only make the required minimum payment, depending on the interest rate (e.g. 18%), you may be paying around $75.00 towards interest and $35.00 towards the principal balance.

At the end of the year, you would have paid $420 towards the principal and $900 towards the interest. It would take approximately 144 months/12 years to pay off the original $5,000. Also, you could pay approx. $10,800 in interest over those 144 months in addition to the original $5,000 principal amount. Total payback $15,800 just for charging $5,000. And this is just for one card:

- $75 per month to interest=$900 per year, $35 per month to principal=$420 per year
- $5,000 divided by $420 (annual principal payment) = 12 years = 144 months
- $900 (annual interest payment) times 12 years = $10,800
- $5,000 (average principal balance) + $10,800 = $15,800 total payback

Although, this example is for illustration purposes only, it reflects how the credit card payment process works. The final interest total and payback period will depend on when and if you only make minimum payments. You get my point?

Buying things with OPM (on credit) can cause you to have a negative cash flow and stay in debt for many years. While the credit card issuer makes a huge profit from your interest payments.

Default Rate

Do not become a victim of the "default" rate. The default rate causes your preferred interest rate to increase to a much higher percentage rate, thus costing you more money. The default rate can be invoked due to a combination of several things, such as, spending over your credit limit, not paying the minimum payment due, missing a payment, or late payments.

Because your default payment history appears in your credit file, other lenders can use this as justification for increasing your rate. Default rates can go as high as 29.99%, or more depending on the lending institution. With interest rates this high, you could spend thousands of dollars on interest with a minimal decrease in the principal amount owed.

———

In November of 2014, a friend showed me his credit card statement because I was helping him set up to start using my DEBT ELIMINATION ROLLOVER PAYMENT PLAN outlined later in this chapter. Before we got started, I pointed out the late payment warning on his credit statement. It stated, " If we do not receive your minimum payment by the due date listed above you may have to pay a late fee up to $37.00 and your APR may increase up to the Variable Penalty APR of 29.99%. Please note that the standard purchase APR is 16.99%." He was completely unaware of the impact that making late payments will have because he did not read the fine print!

As you can see, when you no longer pay all of your bills on time or at least make the minimum payments, the APR can be raised significantly higher. STOP! Re-read the above two paragraphs before moving on.

By now, you have maxed out all of your credit cards, and you cannot get a bank loan. Payday loans are charging you astronomical interest rates. No family member or friend will extend you any more credit. Also, you are in jeopardy of losing your house and your car as well as a wage garnishment against your paycheck.

Many people are living this scenario right at this very moment. Is your debt holding you back? Personal debt makes one a slave to the material possessions. Long after the newness wears off, the debt is still hanging around reminding you of what you purchased on credit. Is keeping up with the Joneses a reason to get into debt? I don't think so, but so many people try to justify the reason they now live paycheck to paycheck.

Some people are in thousands of dollars of debt while others are in millions of dollars of debt. Some small countries owe billions, and the United States of America is in trillions of dollars of debt. As you can see, you are not standing alone on the issue of debt. The question is, what are you going to do about it?

DEBT MISMANAGEMENT FACTORS

In order to begin and continue to manage your debt, you must be aware of the many common factors that lead to debt mismanagement resulting in poor credit. See how many of the factors below reflect your situation:

- Irregular payment practices. Making late payments, missing payments, making less than the required minimum amount, compounding late fees, overdraft checking fees and annual cardholder fees are all examples of things to avoid.
- High interest rate car loans. Also, be aware of the impact of the introductory zero payment options (interest rate and no payment) on new vehicles. While a 0% interest rate for example 60 months is great, you might not qualify. You will need really good credit to get a 0% interest rate deal. So be prepared to pay interest, if you want the vehicle.

  Some dealers may offer you a "no payment for XX months" deal to get you to buy the vehicle. With this offer, after the period ends, you still owe the full loan amount plus accrued interest. And your vehicle depreciated in value as soon as you drove it away from the dealership so you are now upside down in value. If you do get a no payment deal, start making payments (or saving the payment amount) immediately. The good news is that 100% of the payment will go towards reducing the principal during the specified time period.

Also, in both these scenarios, the price of the vehicle may be higher than financed vehicles and not negotiable. The dealer has to make money some way! Be sure you know your credit score before going to the dealership to ensure you get a reasonable interest rate and deal.

- Payday Loans and Cash Advances. Avoid at all cost! They carry much higher interest rates over and above the average credit and loan rates. According to the Center for Responsible Lending, a typical two-week payday loan has an annual interest rate ranging from 391% to 521%. Rates can be upwards of 29.99% or more for cash advances on credit cards.

- Alternative Mortgages. There are some types of mortgages that can cause you to lose your home if you are not aware of the long-term impact. Many start with small down payments and/or mortgage payments but eventually accelerate (balloon) the full balance amount due or significantly increase your mortgage payment (e.g. adjust up). Some only require you to make interest-only payments and never decrease the principal. These types of mortgages should be avoided.

- Home Equity Line of Credit/HELOC. This is a line of credit that is secured by your home and allows you to access money as you need it. The interest rate could be either fixed or variable and is most often tied to the prime rate.

- Education loan. Watch out for the variable rate private loan trap. When you first get approved for the loan, it is affordable, as the variable rate adjusts or increases so does your monthly payments. This can get very costly. If a loan is the only option, stick to the federally backed loans. These tend to allow you to consolidate all your federal loans at a lower fixed rate of interest and offer more repayment options.

- Personal loans to family and friends. This type of loan is very seldom repaid in a timely manner or at all. In most cases if you lend money to a family member or friend, the loan is usually interest-free with no collateral to secure the loan. Don't lend it if you cannot afford to lose it.
- Co-sign a loan for another person. If they don't pay, you are liable for the amount of the loan and you must pay. Sometimes they leave you holding the bag filled with debt that you did not benefit from. Never co-sign for a loan.
- Want Spending versus Need Spending. Buying luxury cars/SUVs, furs, diamonds, vacations, etc., are OK once you are out of debt and have some savings or investments and can afford them.
- Excessive celebrations. Restrain from having over the top birthday parties. Buying an over-abundance of Christmas presents. Having a celebrity-style wedding with a champagne and caviar reception when you have a beer and bean dip budget, starts your new life off in debt. Consider, having a small intimate, inexpensive wedding. Use the money you saved for a down payment on a house or to get both of you out of debt.
- Life changes such as unexpected disability, divorce, separation or death of a spouse. The loss of supporting income from a spouse, paying alimony, or making child support payments or paying legal fees, can add to your debt load.
- Addictions such as alcohol, drugs and gambling can cost you your home, family, job, and in some cases, even your life.

Debt is like an 800-pound gorilla standing on your back. Debt creeps up on you in many different ways. Before you know it, you will wake up one day (or already have) to the fact that this 800-pound gorilla is killing your future. Money is a medium of exchange that passes from one hand to the other, from your employer to you and from you to those you are in debt with. The question is, how much money do you keep?

Think about how much you make, how much you spend on debt and how much of your hard earned money you keep in the form of emergency savings, retirement savings or investments? The less debt you have, the more positive cash flow is available for savings, investing and retirement planning. It is extremely important to understand the goal is to pay little to no interest and no additional fees whatsoever.

You should now have a better understanding of what debt is, how you got into debt and the different factors that cause debt mismanagement. So, let's now look at how to get that 800-pound gorilla called debt off of your back, once and for all.

STEPS TO GET OUT OF DEBT

To get out of debt, you must first admit to yourself that you have a debt problem and that your debt is out of control. Your debt is costly and you want to get out of it. Even though you have income, you let your outgo exceed it, which caused your upkeep to become your downfall. You no longer have enough positive cash flow to pay all your bills on time.

All of a sudden, the lavish lifestyle with all the expensive material things you purchased on credit using Mr. Visa or Mrs. MasterCard or Uncle American Express is no longer fun. Because of delinquent payments your credit is bad along with your credit score.

You wanted help and you had nowhere to turn. But now that you know what debt is and what mismanagement factors may have attributed to your debt to begin with, here are some debt management steps you can take to get yourself out of debt.

Use the six steps below to help you get started just like my friend did back in November 2014. You will be surprised how much you will find out about your personal finances. Maybe for the first time in your life you are looking at your actual financial snapshot. Financially Speaking, this information can assist you in changing from being a wandering generality to becoming a meaningful specific when it comes to your personal financial change.

Step 1 – Balance and Reconcile Your Checking Account Regularly.

Step 2 – Create a Debt/Expense Statement – list all debts, expenses and their due dates.

Step 3 – Create an Income Statement – list all sources of income and dates received.

Step 4 – Calculate Your Cash Flow – (the difference between your income and expenses)-is it Positive or Negative?

Step 5A – If Negative Cash Flow – Begin Expense Elimination Reduction Action Plan.

Step 5B – If Negative Cash Flow – Begin Debt Elimination Rollover Payment Plan.

If you have a <u>Positive Cash Flow</u>, start a Saving Plan to provide cash for investing and/or expedite the Debt Elimination Rollover Payment Plan. See Chapter 3-Net Worth and Chapter 4-Building Wealth: Create A Legacy for more options.

Let's take a closer look at each step listed above.

Step 1 – Balance and Reconcile Your Checking Account Regularly

Balancing and reconciling your checking account is one of the most important first steps in debt management. It is the best and most efficient way of keeping track of how much you are spending on your debts, living expenses, and other items on a daily and monthly basis. Your checking account statement and check (transaction) register are the two tools you can use to help facilitate this process.

You must document all financial transactions going into and coming out of your checking account to absolutely without fail, always know down to the exact penny how much available cash is on hand. You will be able to use the information in your register and monthly statement to help determine your positive or negative cash flow which is the common denominator needed for use in the remaining steps.

In the days before personal computers, cell phones, and tablets, balancing and reconciling your checking account was primarily a manual paper-based activity. However, you can now access your checking account information immediately online or from a broad range of Checkbook Balancing apps available on your cell phone and tablets. Your financial institution's Online Banking application is a convenient way to monitor your transaction activity and access your current account balance 24 hours a day.

It is just as important for you to keep a hard (electronic) copy, for your records, of your daily financial transactions and balances in your check register and your monthly/quarterly/ annual statements. This will also save you time during tax filing season by having a record of all your financial transactions for the year.

Before using any online app, you should understand how to balance and reconcile. Even if you don't actually carry a checkbook, you still need to balance and reconcile your account. Even if you don't have a checking account and only use cash, you should get in the habit of keeping a record of how much you are spending and on what each month.

Learning how to balance and reconcile your account is easy. It only takes a few extra minutes each month and helps you:

- Develop good money management habits
- Keep track of your money and what you are spending it on
- Catch mistakes made by you and/or the bank
- Avoid "overdrafts" and associated fees caused by spending money you don't have in your account

Below is an example of a paper check register. It may look a little different in the various apps, but the information required to balance and reconcile is the same:

TABLE 2.1-CHECK REGISTER SAMPLE

Number or Transaction	Date	Transaction Description	Payment Amount	Deposit Amount	Balance
					$5,015.25
DB	10/01/2015	Walgreen	$20.00		$4,995.25
DP	10/10/2015	Check from Friend		$100.12	$5,095.37
ATM	10/10/2015	Starbucks	$5.43		$5,089.94
Debit	10/10/2015	Taco Bell	$7.03		$5,082.91
1000	10/13/2015	Car Payment	$534.98		$4,547.93
AD	10/13/2015	Payroll		$1,000.00	$5,547.93
Debit	10/15/2015	Chili's	$22.35		$5,525.58
Debit	10/17/2015	Staples	$55.50		$5,470.08
TRF	10/18/2015	Transfer From Savings		$65.00	$5,535.08
BP	10/18/2015	Visa	$58.60		$5,476.48
ATM	10/18/2015	Gas	$5.80		$5,470.68
TRF	10/22/2015	Transfer To Savings	$65.00		$5,405.68
1001	10/23/2015	Target	$120.65		$5,285.03
AD	10/31/2015	Payroll		$1,000.00	$6,285.03
AW	11/01/2015	Rent	$750.00		$5,535.03

AD Automatic Deposit — AW Automatic Withdrawal — ATM Automatic Teller — BP Bill Payment — DB Debit — DP Deposit — TRF Transfer

Here are the basic steps to follow at the beginning, throughout and at the end of each month:

1. **Record** - start your check register by recording the "Starting Balance". In the upper right-hand corner of the above check register sample, you will see $5,015.25 as the ending balance on September 30th the last day of the month. It becomes the beginning balance on October 1st.

   At the beginning of each month (October for this example) locate your prior month's ending balance using your checking account statement, checkbook balancing app or your checkbook register. Write this balance at the top of your check register or enter in the proper place within the app.

2. **Track** - your transaction activity daily. Write down and record every transaction you make immediately or as soon as possible in your check register or app register. That includes check purchases, ATM card purchases, ATM cash withdrawals, deposits, purchase refunds and known fees. You should record:

   a. check number, if applicable or short description (e.g. ATM, Debit, etc.)

    b. transaction date

    c. long description – April mortgage payment, school supplies, clothes, dinner, fee. This makes it easier to trace if a discrepancy occurs

    d. withdrawal/debit amount

    e. deposit/credit amount

    f. balance (running) after transaction

3. **Post** - as you post each transaction, calculate your new running daily balance. Subtract the amount of each of your withdrawals, purchases, returned check deposits, electronic debits (e.g. automatic bill payments) and known fees from the existing running balance or prior month's ending balance. Also, add the amount of each of your personal deposits, electronic deposits (e.g. paycheck) and purchase refunds to the balance. Continue this process daily throughout the month.

4. **Review** - after the end of the month, you should receive a statement from your financial institution or go online to review your transaction history for the month. The statement/history will contain:

    a. the statement period (usually 1st to last day of the month)

    b. your prior month's ending balance

    c. your transaction activity and bank assessed fees (e.g. overdrafts) along with daily running balances

    d. the current statement's month ending balance (this will become next month's prior ending balance).

5. **Reconcile** - start your reconcilement. Compare your check register or app transactions and ending balance to the statement. If they match, you have accounted for all of your transactions for that month. Great Job! You are now balanced and reconciled for the month! Make a notation next to the ending balance in your register to indicate that it balanced on MM/DD/YYYY. This helps you to know the last time your check register balanced with your checking account.

6. **Research** - if they don't match, there are some things to check:

   a. Look at the statement to see if there are transactions on it that you did not record such as fees, missed purchases, electronic debits or deposits, etc. If yes, and you know you made them or are applicable, apply them to your register. If your register is now balanced, Great Job!

   b. If your register is still out of balance, compare each transaction and running balance in your register to your statement. Ensure the transaction amounts are the same and you calculated the running balances correctly. I know on many occasions, I have transposed numbers as I entered transactions in my register. Also, check that the prior month's balance you used was correct. Make any necessary adjustments to your register. If your register is now balanced, Great Job!

   c. If your register is still not balanced or you find transactions on your statement that you don't understand or didn't make, contact your financial institution immediately for assistance. This will help you discover any unauthorized transactions by another party. Work with your financial institution until all items are resolved so that you can get back in balance with your register and your financial institution.

There are two other significant balances that you should understand when viewing your account information or verifying that you have sufficient funds to make a purchase. They are your Ledger Balance and Available Balance. These two balances are critical to avoiding overdrawing your account and incurring significant fees.

- **<u>Ledger Balance</u>** reflects <u>all</u> of the transaction activity that your financial institution posted to your account the prior night even if the funds have not cleared.

What this means is, for example, you deposit a $100.00 Citibank check into your US Bank account. The check amount will be posted to your ledger balance even though Citibank has not yet transferred the money to US Bank.

- **Available Balance** reflects how much of the ledger balance you can actually withdraw or use for purchase at the moment. In the above example, US Bank will not make the $100.00 available to you for anywhere from 1 to 10 days. Therefore, you need to rely on the **Available** Balance in determining how much you can spend. Not the Ledger Balance.

Step 2 – Create a Debt and Expense Statement

To start your get out of debt plan of action, you first must be honest with yourself and determine how much debt you really have and how much you are spending on a monthly basis. You might be alarmed once all the numbers are totaled. This is much simpler for a single person who handles his or her own bills. You just make a list of all your debts and expenses.

For married couples or couples who have individual and joint debt together with expenditures, this could be a challenge. If one spouse or significant other hides or has no knowledge of any amount of debt from the other, your personal debt management rebuilding process will take longer than expected. Both of you should be accountable to each other when it comes to the total household income, expenses, and debt.

There is a difference between a debt and an expense. Debt is a legal obligation that you owe to others in the form of credit (OPM). While expenses are daily expenditures on items needed for basic living and upkeep or just on things, you need and want. It is important to list all your debts separately from your expenses along with their due dates.

Add up all your debt and expenses for a monthly total. List the following information for each of your debts and recurring expenses:

- creditor name
- type of debt/expense (e.g. mortgage, utility-gas, student loan, credit card, food)
- payment frequency (e.g. monthly, quarterly)
- payment due date
- payment amount
- interest rate
- months remaining to pay off, if applicable

Later, if you need to call your creditors and negotiate things like lower interest rates or no late payment fees, you will have all the information right at your fingertips. Reminder, you cannot effectively manage your debt without a complete and accurate list of all your debt.

Examples of things to list on your debt statement are:

- credit cards
- loans - (students, payday, installment, auto, and personal).
- mortgages – (primary and secondary)
- equity credit line
- alimony/child support payments

Examples of things to list on your expense statement:

- rent
- utilities
- cell phone bill
- home telephone bill
- cable bill
- groceries
- auto, homeowners or renters insurance
- vehicle maintenance
- vehicle license plates and window stickers
- internet service
- personal transportation expense (weekly gas bills, tolls)
- public transportation expense (cash or transit card cost)
- lawn care service
- snow removal service

- garbage pickup
- hair and nails
- dry cleaning
- clothes
- child/adult day care
- daily coffee, latté or tea
- cigarettes
- health care
- children's extracurricular activities (e.g. dance, piano, sports)
- dining out (e.g. McDonalds, Rib Joint, Steak Joint, Baskin Robbins)
- lottery tickets

Step 3 – Create an Income Statement

List all sources and date of income that you receive on a monthly basis. This will help you line up your income with your debt and expense payment due dates. Total income from all sources for one month. Include all income sources, for example:

- income from your full and/or part-time jobs
- passive income (rental property)
- active income (buy, rehab and resale real estate).
- alimony and child support (either you are the payee or the receiver)
- tips or gratuities
- public assistance (one can pull him or herself up by their bootstraps regardless of present situation)
- pension
- Social Security
- annuities amounts
- retirement plans - 401k- 457
- stocks, bonds, mutual funds, other investments
- home-based business income

Step 4 – Calculate Your Cash Flow

To calculate your monthly cash flow, use the total income amount for the month from your income statement. Use the total debt/expense amount for the month from your debt/ expense statement. Subtract your total debts and expenses from your income. If the result is a negative number, you have a negative cash flow. Which means you have no money left over at the end of each month. If the result is a positive number, you have a positive cash flow with money left over at the end of each month.

Positive Cash Flow Example:

- Monthly household income total is $5,500.
- Monthly household debt and expense total is $4,000.

As you can see from this example, this household has a positive cash flow of $1,500 ($5,500 (income) - $4,000 (debt/ expenses) = $1,500). This means you have cash flow available to start building wealth (review Chapter 4-Building Wealth for ways to best utilize your positive cash flow). Or you can choose to accelerate paying off your debts or expenses first-See Step 5A & 5B.

Negative Cash Flow Example:

- Monthly household income total is $5,500.
- Monthly household expense and debt total are $6,000.

As you can see from this example, this household has a negative cash flow of $500 ($5,500 (income) - $6,000 (debt/ expenses) = -$500). This means some of the bills are being paid late or not all.

"You should carefully read Steps 5A and 5B below if you have a negative cash flow."

Step 5A – Expense Reduction Plan

Now that you can actually see where your money goes and how much you are short each month, you can make some changes. What expenses will you cut that will bridge the financial gap of disparity between your income and expenses? You have some hard, tough choices ahead. Personal discipline will be a must if you really want to lower your debt, increase your positive cash flow, start eliminating your debt and begin the road to transforming your Financial DNA For Life. You can work overtime on your present job or get a second job and apply that extra money toward getting out of debt.

Another option is to find ways to reduce or eliminate some of your expenses. I purchased chicken and fish in bulk once a month. I baked the chicken and fish every week and took it for lunch along with apples, bananas, grapes and nuts for years. I saved quite a bit of money by not buying lunch at fast food restaurants every day. I also was able to maintain my weight by eating healthy.

My wife, reluctantly, started getting her hair and nails done once a month instead of weekly. She also agreed to no new shoes for six months LOL. This saved a lot of money over a period of time all of which she used to pay down her personal debt.

Review your list of expenses and decide which of the outgoing expenditures you can eliminate to help free up the $500 needed to change your negative cash flow to break even, from the example above. This might be the most difficult way of getting out of debt because no one wants to cut back on the comforts and luxuries that make life more enjoyable.

You can reduce your spending by giving up your car, or reducing the number of times you dine out monthly or do your own manicures and pedicures. The fact remains, that if you take the time to put your outgoing expenses in writing you will be able to see where the money is going and where you can make the needed cutbacks.

Expense Management Tips

There are numerous debt management concepts you may want to consider that can help reduce or eliminate your debts and expenses:

- You can set up an on-line bill payment system. You can have your bills paid automatically from your checking account directly to your creditors on or before the due dates. This will eliminate late payments and associated fees. You will have an electronic payment history; you can pay bills 24 hours a day, 7 days a week. This also will save you the cost of stamps and envelopes.

- Stop spending on unnecessary things; determine your needs versus wants.
- Reduce the number of times you go to the barber/hair salon or the manicurist on a monthly basis (e.g. instead of weekly go twice or once a month).
- If you use revolving credit, pay the balance off in full every payment cycle to avoid interest payments.
- Pay with cash or debit cards if at all possible. Cash and carry purchasing always leaves you with no more additional debt.
- Drink regular coffee instead of latte or cappuccino from your favorite coffee shop. Better yet, buy a coffee maker with an automatic timer and purchase your favorite coffee by the pound and make it at home. You will save quite a bit on a monthly basis.
- Brown bags it for lunch: If you buy lunch every day add up the total cost, times five to see how much per week you spend. Don't forget about the daily coffee (e.g. Starbucks), donut, muffin or croissant for breakfast. This could add up to major savings. Example; if you spend $6 per day for lunch (like I once did), you spend a total of $30 ($6 X 5 days) per week. As of September, 2nd 2015, a Big Mack meal cost $5.99, Whopper meal cost $6.09 and a Chipotle Chicken Burrito/Bowl cost $6.95 in Chicago.

  Now $30 X 52 weeks equals $1,560 per year in lunch. Over the next five years, you will spend at least $7,800 for lunch-OMG! If you spend more than $6 per day on lunch and include breakfast, which most people do, you will spend closer to $10,000 per year. Making the change from eating lunch at restaurants to bringing your lunch to work will allow you to free up some additional cash.

- Stop unnecessary driving: with the price of gas being unpredictable, personal consumption should be kept to a minimum. This will allow you to save even more when the price of gas drops. The AAA Daily Fuel Gauge Report indicated that in September 2015, the National average of one gallon of regular gas cost $2.447 cents. While the same period in 2014 found the same gallon was approximately one dollar more at $3.434 cents per gallon. This is an excellent time to sock away the savings that you are receiving at the pump while gas prices are still low.

- Carpool or use public transportation: Split the expenses between all the riders which will save on parking fees, gas, and vehicle maintenance. By using public transportation, with the different fare structures available, you can find the one that fits into your transportation needs as well as a possible reduction in your overall transportation costs.
- Raise the deductible on your car and home/renter insurance to lower your monthly premium payments.
- Wash and wear more. Dry clean less.
- Cut your own grass or shovel your own snow, instead of paying someone. Do this only if your health permits. If you need to pay someone, hire a neighborhood kid. I am sure they and their parents would appreciate the extra income.
- Shop at discount and thrift stores. You can find many good quality brand name items at discount prices.
- Sell unwanted items on eBay, at flea markets, or garage sales for extra money.
- Stop gambling: Are you a casino king or queen without the wealth? Do you take your hard earned paycheck to the casino or riverboat in hopes of hitting it big? When you lose your paycheck, do you resort to getting cash advances with interest rates around 18% to 20% or higher? What about the lottery or the race track for dogs or horses or off-track betting parlors. Now with internet gambling, you don't even need to leave home to drain your finances. Seek professional help if your gambling is out of control.
- Stop smoking. It's not good for your health and your wealth because cigarettes are expensive. Take the cost

of cigarettes, multiply by how many packs you buy every week and discover how much money you can save. According to a September 27th, 2014, article by The Motley Fool, the estimated average cost of a pack of cigarettes in Illinois was $11.50. If you smoke two packs per week at $11.50 per pack, that's around $92.00 per month and $1,104 per year. That's over $1,000 a year in saving if you STOP smoking!

- Stop using credit cards. The longer you use them, the longer you will stay in debt and the more interest you will pay. If you purchase on credit, pay the balance in full every month. Do not carry credit card debt unless it has a zero percent interest rate.

- Do not make late payments on your credit cards. At least make the minimum payment on time to avoid late fees and default charges. Some credit card companies charge a late payment fee for a certain amount of debt. Example: If you make a late payment and the balance is $250 or less you might be charged $19.00 in late fees. If the balance is over $250 and you make a late payment you might be charged $39.00. The fees charged will vary from company to company. As you can see, making late payments deducts available cash that could go toward reducing your debt and investing for your future. Pay more than the minimum amount due. This will reduce the outstanding principal balance faster.

- Don't pay annual fees. Some credit cards will charge you an annual fee per the terms of their agreement. The average fee can range from $25.00 up $75.00, but some are even higher. The money you pay in annual fees could be better spent, to lower your debt. There are credit card issuers that offer no annual fee. Seek them out. (See Appendix for credit card resources).

- Don't spend over your approved credit limit. Over the credit limit fees can be $35.00 or more depending on the lending institution.

- Do not obtain cash advances on your credit cards. You can be charged up to 25% or higher interest and fees depending on the card issuer.

- Unless your child is a true prodigy/real talent, stop spending a fortune on piano lessons, dance classes, and sports activities. There are many free extracurricular activities they can get involved in. It doesn't make you a bad parent just a smart, realistic one. Once your child shows a real interest or talent, then invest in them.
- Research lower rates for your car, home, and medical insurance. However, don't sacrifice quality for price. Your life and safety are priceless.

Now that you have some tips on how to identify and reduce your expenses, the next crucial step in learning debt management is how to eliminate your debt using "The Debt Elimination Rollover Payment Plan," outlined next in step 5B below.

Step 5B – Debt Elimination Rollover Payment Plan

How can you swim in the waters of financial
freedom,
when you are drowning in a deep sea of debt?
-MICHAEL BART MATHEWS

You can work at paying off your debt sooner by creating a Debt Elimination Rollover Payment Plan. Under this plan, you can use the total amount of money you are currently spending on all of your monthly bills to get out of debt sooner. The way it works is to eliminate one bill at a time, roll over the amount of the payment on the bill that was paid in full to the next bill, and then continuing this process until you are out of debt - see Table 2.2 Debt Rollover Payment Plan Chart. This method will automatically increase each subsequent payment amount and ensure that you definitely get out of debt many months, if not years, sooner without needing additional cash. Also negotiating lower interest rates will help expedite your debt elimination plan.

Once that first bill is paid, you might want to justify going out and buying something new and forget about sticking to the debt elimination rollover payment plan. A one-time reward or treat is ok, but stick to the plan and do not quit!

Instead of going on a new spending spree, once you pay off a bill, just use discipline and keep on with your rollover payments. Just add the new found cash flow to the next bill. Self-management and discipline will be key factors for you to succeed in this undertaking.

You will need discipline to get out of debt. You have what it takes, but you must want to get out of debt once and for all. Instead of talking the talk, the goal is to walk the get-out-of-debt walk toward financial freedom by using the Debt Elimination Rollover Payment Plan.

In the example below, I will illustrate the plan. This plan will work regardless if you are paying 0% or 18% interest (negotiate lower interest rates) rate on your open accounts. However by paying 0% or the lowest interest rate possible, you will speed up the length of time it takes to become debt free.

In this illustration, pay attention to the starting minimum payment due on all six debts. As the first debt is eliminated, the minimum payment of the first debt is rolled over to (i.e. increases) the payment amount of second or next debt. You continue the roll-over payment process until you are debt-free. Study the chart below and read how the process works, then you will be ready to start your own plan.

Table 2.2 Debt Rollover Payment Plan Chart

Debts	STARTING Minimum Monthly Payment	New Monthly Payment after each Rollover	Outstanding Balance	Number of Months at Minimum	Number of Months to Repayment
#1.CREDIT CARD	$100.00	$0	$3,000	30	30
#2.CREDIT CARD	$125.00	$225.00	$5,000	40	35
#3.CREDIT CARD	$150.00	$375.00	$7,000	47	37
#4.STUDENT LOAN	$400.00	$775.00	$15,000	38	38
#5.AUTO LOAN	$500.00	$1,275.00	$18,000	36	36
#6.MORTGAGE	$900.00	$2,175.00	$120,000	134	78
TOTAL DEBTS	$2,175.00		$168,000		

This is how the plan works; you will continue to make the minimum payments on each of the debts listed above until all debts are paid. Let's say you just made your last payment on debt #1, the first credit card bill of $100.00 per month. It took 30 months to eliminate this debt. Next, add or rollover the $100.00 payment from the first bill, to your second bill, debt #2, the second credit card. Now you are paying $225.00 towards this bill resulting in a 5-month early payoff.

Now that your first two debts are eliminated repeat the rollover debt reduction process by adding or rolling over the total amount of the first two payments to debt #3, the 3rd credit card bill. Now you are paying a total of $375.00 instead of $150.00. By paying $375.00, it will take you around 37 months to pay off this same debt instead of 47. Ten months less.

Now, that you have eliminated the first three bills on your list you can now finish debt #4, the Student Loan. In this case, after 37 months the Student Loan bill only had one $400.00 payment left. Also, debt#5, the Car Payment was paid off in 36 months.

We are now in the home stretch with final debt #6, the mortgage payment. Keep up your discipline and watch how quickly you can pay off your home. The total amount of your five eliminated debts equals $1,275.00. Add this amount to your current $900.00 per month mortgage payment for a total of $2,175.00. You now apply this total towards your monthly mortgage to pay it off faster. You are actually using the same debt total you started the plan with, which illustrates, you can get out of debt using your current income.

Finally by using the Debt Elimination Rollover Payment Plan, you will pay off your mortgage in around 77 months (instead of 134), a reduction of almost half the time. You will save an enormous amount of interest using this rollover payment plan.

For this illustration only, if you stick to the plan, you can be debt free in about six years and 4 months (instead of 11 years) including paying off your home mortgage. It should be noted that a zero percent interest rate was used. Few people pay zero percent on all of their debt. However, it points out that you do have a way out of debt using the exact same amount of monthly income you are currently receiving.

Depending on the rate of interest (APR) on each of your debts, you will need to factor in the interest amount and the outstanding principal. This will give you a more realistic determination of when you will finish your Debt Elimination Rollover Payment Plan.

Take a closer look at your income and expense statements and find more savings by cutting back on spending or working overtime hours on your current job or getting a part-time job. You can use the additional income toward eliminating your debts. No matter what plan you decide to use, for it to work, you must remain focused until you have reduced, and then finally eliminated your debt.

Other Debt Management Tips

There are a couple more debt management tips you can use to help reduce or eliminate your debts:

1. Zero Percent Rate Credit Cards Offers-Pros and Cons

PROS: Pay particular attention to the zero percent interest rate credit card balance transfer offers you receive in the mail. If used responsibly, this could be an excellent way to save on interest payments, and lower your debt at the same time.

For example, you have a debt and the monthly payment is $100.00 per month. Of that amount, $75.00 goes toward interest and $25.00 goes toward the outstanding principal balance. Now, you transfer the balance from the debt that is charging you $75.00 in interest to a zero percent rate card. Let's say the terms for the zero percent card last only 12 months. If you keep paying the same $100.00 on the zero percent interest rate card, all of your payments will go toward the outstanding principal balance for at least one year. Now, $1,200 ($100.00 X 12 months) is going directly toward the unpaid balance instead of $300 ($25.00 X 12 months). Thus, you will reduce your debt at an accelerated rate.

Just before the zero percent rate card offer expires, you once again transfer the balance to another zero percent rate card. Continue to make the exact same principal payment to take advantage of zero percent for another 12 months or whatever the length of the terms are.

CONS: for this to work you cannot add any additional debt to the zero percent interest rate cards. If you do, you could be charged high interest, and that is what you want to avoid. Also, you should make the minimum payment required, and make all payments on time, to help ensure you retain your zero percent rate status. Be aware of the balance transfer fees. Make sure they are reasonable before doing the transfer. Also, do not fall into the zero percent on purchases trap. Why? You can accumulate a large amount of outstanding debt at zero percent for 12 months. On the 13th month, the zero percent can increase to high double-digit interest rates. Now you are right back at square one with high interest payments! Discipline is a crucial factor in using zero percent rate credit cards.

Your credit card statement comes with the following mandated information, for example:

- Late Payment Warning- up to $35.00 late fee (sometimes more) will be accessed and your APRs may be increased up to the Penalty APR of 29.99% if the minimum payment is not received by the payment due date.
- Minimum Payment Warning- If you only make the Total Minimum Payment each period, you will pay more in interest and it will take you longer to pay off your balance. For example: For a $9,882 credit card balance with a 9.99% interest rate, you would pay off the balance in 23 years for a total of $17,501. WOW!

Due to these mandated warnings, the credit card companies have relieved themselves of unfair credit practices by putting the sole burden of credit management, repayment, and responsibility squarely in your hands. In the end, you, not the credit card companies, is responsible for your credit worthiness or lack thereof.

Credit card companies are trying to give the public the perception that they are helping you use your cards responsibly. However, the many different promotional offers like zero percent on purchases and zero percent on balance transfers for an expressed period of time are all designed to get you to use the cards. Once the introductory period is over, high interest rates ranging between 8.99% to 29.99% or more kick in. If you make one late payment while you are still in the zero percent introductory rate period, you could lose that zero percent and automatically start paying the higher interest rates. Now you can beat them at their own game.

2. *Amortization Schedules*

Order the amortization schedules from the lender when you take out a loan. It will contain the original loan amount, the interest rate, the length of the loan (number of months) and the monthly payment amount. It includes how much of the monthly payment goes toward the principal and how much goes toward the interest. It will also show how much you will pay in total interest over the life of the loan.

Below is an example of how using an amortization schedule allowed me to save thousands of dollars of interest on just one of my accounts.

Example: Original loan amount $26,910.00
   Interest rate 12%
   Length of loan 120 months (Ten Years)
   First payment 04/10/2005
   Last Payment 03/10/2015

The monthly payment amount was $386.08. Of this amount, $116.98 went toward the principal and $269.10 went toward interest for the 1st month. For the subsequent months, the amount applied toward the principal increases around $1.00 to $2.00. The total amount of interest I would have paid over the life of the loan was approximately $19,400.00. Once I saw how much I was spending on interest, I used the information from the amortization schedule to negotiate a lower interest rate. I was successful in getting the rate down from 12% to 5%.

The magic of debt reduction happened when I kept paying the $386.08 original minimum payment at the lower 5% rate. This enabled me to pay more toward the principal amount. Therefore, my debt was reduced at a faster pace saving me thousands of dollars, almost $12,100 in total interest. I also paid an additional amount per month above the minimum payment directly to the principal amount resulting in further interest savings and a faster payoff. Recap; negotiating lower interest rates and making additional payments can save you a significant sum of money.

In order for you to do-it-yourself, look at your loan documents and input the amount of the loan, interest rate, loan term and repayment start date into an amortization calculator (you can find one online) and get the schedule yourself. You can request your amortization schedule to be emailed or mailed from your lender.

Once you receive this information, you can decide to make additional repayment amounts to shorten the length of time you will be in debt. Amortization schedules work for mortgages, credit cards, car notes, student loan or any kind of debt.

CREATE A SPENDING PLAN

Because you should already know all of your income sources, expenses, and debts, you can begin to track and control your spending and cash flow by creating a SPENDING PLAN (aka budget). I know that budgets have gotten a bad rap because it makes you feel like you are limiting your choices and depriving yourself. That is because that is how you were taught.

A spending plan helps you take control of your finances as you distinguish between your (needs and wants). With a spending plan, you will track your expenditures and total them by category each month. This will allow you to see how much you are spending on food, entertainment, transportation, clothes, etc. Use your debt/expense statement and your income statement to create your spending plan. Create a spending plan for each month, containing what you expect to spend on needs and wants. See sample below.

After you reconcile your checking account and receive your credit card statements for the month, record the totals of what you actually spent. Be sure to add the items that were not initially accounted for in the spending plan. Subtract the "planned spend amount" from the "actual amount spent". The difference is either a surplus that can be used to pay down debt or to save; or a shortage meaning you spent more than you planned. Evaluate each item causing the shortage and determine if it was a need, want or I could have lived without. You will need to make adjustments to next month's plan to account for the shortage.

My wife and I decided to get back into the habit of creating a spending plan. We dumped all of our checking and credit card transactions into a spreadsheet and totaled our expenditures by category for the first seven months in 2015. What we discovered, was an OMG revelation. We spent close to $7,000 on groceries and dining out. I guess you can say we were really "eating high off the hog, the cow and the chicken"!! If we hadn't created the spending plan, we would not have discovered this. We made adjustments to our eating habits without depriving ourselves of the things we really like. We were able to save approx. $500 per month in unnecessary food expense.

Your spending plan will allow you to make adjustments to your spending as well as closely track your cash flow or lack of it. You will be surprised just how much money you can save if you focus your spending on your (needs) and plan occasional treats (wants) for yourself. Instant gratification contributes to costly financial overspending.

In reviewing the Table 2.3 Spending Plan sample below, you can see in the Monthly Surplus or Shortage row at the bottom that you spent $456 more than your total income for the month. When this happens, you must review the "actual spend" column to see why you went over budget and make the necessary changes to your spending habits. Create your own plan. Give it a try for a couple of months and see for yourself how helpful and eye opening it can be. You should also follow the recommendations in Steps 5A and 5B to reduce/eliminate your debts.

TABLE 2.3 SPENDING PLAN (BUDGET) SAMPLE

Spending Plan (Budget) Worksheet			
Month: January			
	Planned Spend	Actual Spend	Difference
Income			
Salary #1	1,500.00	1,500.00	0.00
Salary #2	1,200.00	1,200.00	0.00
Tips/Bonus			
Other Income			
Total Income	$ 2,700.00	$ 2,700.00	$ -
Expenses			
Savings Account			0.00
Retirement (401k, IRA)			0.00
College			0.00
Savings Total	0.00	0.00	0.00
Mortgage / Rent	600.00	600.00	0.00
Electricity	50.00	60.00	(10.00)
Gas	25.00	20.00	5.00
Water/Sewer	50.00	80.00	(30.00)
Cable/Internet	100.00	100.00	0.00
Garbage			0.00
Maintenance/Repairs			0.00
Housing Total	825.00	860.00	(35.00)
Car Payment #1	300.00	300.00	0.00
Car Payment #2	400.00	400.00	0.00
Bus/Train/Taxi Fare			0.00
Insurance	500.00	500.00	0.00
Fuel	150.00	250.00	(100.00)
Maintenance			0.00
Transportation Total	1,350.00	1,450.00	(100.00)
Groceries	150.00	175.00	(25.00)
Dining Out	50.00	75.00	(25.00)
Food Total	200.00	250.00	(50.00)
Tuition/Fees			0.00
Books/Supplies			0.00
Room/Board			0.00
Student Loan #1			0.00
Student Loan #2			0.00
Education Total	0.00	0.00	0.00
Credit Cards #1	100.00	96.00	4.00
Credit Cards #2	100.00	125.00	(25.00)
Other			0.00
Other Loans Total	200.00	221.00	(21.00)
Childcare expenses			0.00
Beauty (Hair/Nails)		50.00	(50.00)
Clothing			0.00
Dry Cleaning		0.00	0.00
Gym	25.00	25.00	0.00
Other			0.00
Personal Total	25.00	75.00	(50.00)
Movies			0.00
Concerts/Theater		200.00	(200.00)
Sporting Events			0.00
Other			0.00
Entertainment Total	0.00	200.00	(200.00)
Home / Rent	50.00	50.00	0.00
Health	50.00	50.00	0.00
Life			0.00
Other			0.00
Insurance Total	100.00	100.00	0.00
Donations			0.00
Charitable Giving Total	0.00	0.00	0.00
Food/Grooming/Medical			0.00
Pets Total	0.00	0.00	0.00
Total Monthly Expenses	2,700.00	3,156.00	(456.00)
Monthly Surplus or Shortage	0.00	(456.00)	
(Total Income - Total Monthly Expenses)			

STUDENT LOAN DEBT-TURNING COLLEGE DREAMS INTO NIGHTMARES

It is important that I address the next biggest debt issue facing millions of parents and children now and in the future. As parents, we all dreamed of a better life for our children, just as our parents did for us. We have visions of our children attending a prestigious college or university, graduating as doctors, lawyers or with other prominent careers. We were eager to sign all types of student loan applications to ensure our children realized our/their dreams. It was an investment based on the prospect of higher future income for our children.

As we are now realizing, those dreams are turning into student loan repayment nightmares. Student loan debt has reached an all-time high of $1.2 trillion (USD) United States Dollars. It's the second largest form of household debt among consumers after mortgages.

As a result of the recession, lucrative employment opportunities for college graduates disappeared in most all fields and many parents lost their jobs as well. Many college graduates are working minimum wage or entry level jobs while looking for higher paying, career orientated positions. This has put paying back student loans very low on the priority list behind, food, shelter and clothing. It is also negatively impacting the credit scores of both the parent and the student, depending on who's name the loan is in.

It is a major area of concern within the academic, Main Street, Wall Street, and political arenas. The government has made numerous policy attempts at easing the financial burden for students and the nation's economy overall. On June 9th, 2014, a presidential memorandum was issued regarding the expansion of the "Pay as You Earn" (PAYE) alternative student loan repayment program. This new policy change signaled the severity of the student loan crisis for both the government and borrowers who struggle to pay off their education debts.

I am not going to sugar coat this problem. The only thing you can hope for as a student loan debt holder, short of filing for bankruptcy, is to find ways to pay down or pay off your portion of the massive student loan debt. Unlike federal student loans, private student loans repayment options need to be negotiated directly with the lender. If you have both private and federal loans, some lenders may consolidate them together.

While it is possible to have federal or private student loans canceled in bankruptcy, it is extremely difficult. You must file an "adversary" petition as part of your bankruptcy filing. You must show that repayment of the debt "will impose an undue hardship on you and your dependents." Please consult an attorney with expertise in student loan bankruptcy law to determine if this is a viable option for your situation.

There are ways to help make repayment of Federal student loans easier. Be aware of companies offering to assist you with student loan repayment for a fee. The U.S. Department of Education-Federal Student Aid (www.studentaid.ed.gov/sa/repay-loans) or their loan servicers will help you for free.

Federal student loan repayment options include:

- Repayment Plans - there are a number of different repayment plans beyond the standard 10-year repayment plan for your Direct Loans or Federal Family Education Loans (FFEL). Review each plan to see which one works best for your situation.
- Change your payment due date to align payments with your income pay dates.
- Consolidate your Direct Loans so you only have one payment to deal with.
- If you are really unable to pay at a given point in time, request a deferment or forbearance. Depending upon the type of loan you have, interest may continue to accrue during this period.
- Forgiveness/Cancelation/Discharge – There are several circumstances in which you no longer are required to repay your federal student loan. For instance, some or all of your loan could be forgiven in exchange for you performing certain types of service such as teaching or public service. Or the obligation to make further payments on your loan might be discharged based

on specific factors such as your school closing or you became totally and permanently disabled. Be sure to research all the possibilities.

Despite the challenges, it is possible to wake up from the student loan debt nightmare. This will require discipline and sacrificing the newest high-end designer fashions, the latest and greatest cell phones, video games, traveling, every night out at the bar with friends and other instant self-gratification purchases. The way to pay off student loan debt is to use the Debt Reduction Rollover Payment Plan and put as much money as possible towards paying it off.

The last pieces of advice I would like to pass on to future college-bound students and parents. Start saving and planning for college early as possible. Apply for every type of grant or scholarship you are eligible for. There are numerous merit, ethnic, career, gender, income, athletic and even single mother based scholarships available. Be sure to research them all. You will be surprised what you might find that you are able to apply for.

Get a part-time job and save all of the money towards your college expenses. Consider, taking your 100/200 level Science, Technology, Engineering & Math classes at a good local junior college. Generally, tuition costs for junior college classes are lower than that of a four-year institution. Be sure to confirm with your future four-year school of choice that all of your junior college credits are transferable before enrolling. This will ensure a smooth transition from your associate degree as you work toward your undergraduate degree.

To address the high cost of tuition, the City Colleges of Chicago initiated the Chicago Star Scholarship Program effective starting the fall semester, 2015. Students who graduate from a Chicago Public High School with a 3.0 GPA and an ACT score of 17 or better in math and English can pursue an associate's degree at one of seven Chicago City Colleges at no cost. FREE tuition, fees, and books! Qualified students are required to complete the (FAFSA) Free Application for Federal Student Aid. Any financial aid dollars awarded will be applied to the free Chicago Star Scholarship

Program. Waivers will take care of the rest. Visit the website (www.ccc.edu) for information. You should check to see what free educational programs may be available within your city or state.

You may also want to explore establishing a 529 College Savings Plan. A 529 plan is a tax-advantaged savings plan designed to encourage saving for future college expense. Students must attend an accredited college, university or vocational school in the United States as well as some approved foreign universities.

529 plans are legally known as "qualified tuition plans" sponsored by states, state agencies or educational institutions. They are authorized by Section 529 of the Internal Revenue Code. There are two types of 529 plans:

1. Pre-paid – purchase tuition credits at today's rates for future use. These are administered by states or higher education institutions.
2. Savings plan – growth is based upon market performance and is administered by states only.

Distributions from 529 plans can be used for a variety of different expenses:

- tuition and fees
- books and supplies
- room and board if the student is at least a half-time student
- equipment, if required for class

I strongly suggest that you research the 529 pre-paid and saving plans before signing up. You will need to understand the pros and cons associated with both plans.

And lastly, parents, if you are fortunate enough to have retirement savings, please don't use your savings or take out excessive parent loans to finance your child's college education. We all want the best for our children's future, but their future is ultimately their responsibility. Your retirement savings is there to take care of you in your golden years so you don't have to rely on your children or the government. I am speaking from experience as we had to pay off our daughter's student loan in early retirement. Be proactive and work with your children early to plan for college to minimize the longer term costs for both of you.

Summary

Just try one small financial change that I have suggested to begin changing your overall spending habits. Once you see you are spending less and saving more, then you should try one more item suggested on the list. Or come up with some ways of your own and try them. But you must start now if you want to see results sooner, rather than later.

When you accomplish some of the examples mentioned above, you will be well on your way toward financial change. You will have reduced your spending by no longer paying extra fees, as well as reducing your interest rate for additional savings. This may not seem like much, but it is a start. Depending on how high your annual percentage rate is and the amount of interest you are paying, this, in fact, could be significant monthly savings.

Debt can kill your spirit and emotions because you think about your lack of financial freedom all the time. Even your relationship with your significant other might suffer due to arguments, stress and disagreements caused by high debt. You might lose family members and friends because you borrowed money you can't pay back. When you see them, you hide or go the other way, or make up excuses as to why you can't pay them back. Now you feel all alone because you have no one else to turn to.

One of the worst financial burdens is to have out-of-control debt due to personal mismanagement or circumstances that are sometimes beyond your control. It is not a nice feeling when you get your paycheck and you pay everyone except yourself. Only you can take responsibility for your actions and say once and for all, "Enough is Enough." Decide that you will no longer tolerate unnecessary debt. Whatever your current debt situation is, you can change it by ending bad spending habits that got you into debt in the first place.

Warning; if your debt is growing like deadly cancer eating away at your positive cash flow, you must operate now or you will remain indefinitely in the overcrowded debtors high interest rate payments critical care unit.

There are many ways to accomplish debt reduction that leads to debt elimination. List your debts and expenses with the balances and payment amounts to see the big picture. Chart your expense reduction and start your Debt Elimination Rollover Payment Plan.

Whatever your amount of debt, if you develop a realistic plan of action and practice a strong discipline and a burning desire to become debt-free, you can actually dig yourself out of debt. You must change how you think, act and feel about money!

If you don't have the discipline to do it alone, there are professional financial planners who can serve as your coach to assist and guide you through the process-see Chapter 8-Financial Planning. Also, visit my website (www.tmeginc. com) for additional resources to assist you in getting out of debt.

REMEMBER, "THE BEST IMPROVEMENT STARTS WITH SELF IMPROVEMENT."

POEM - PRESS ON

You are deep in debt, and you want to cry
You call your creditors, and then you try
To lower your payments, and reduce your debt
Because if you don't, they won't get a check
Press on with your calls, and try to lower
The high interest rates, reducing debts slower
Press on with your plan, and you will see
How easy your debt reduction can be
Press on with your plan, because you can
Give yourself, a helping hand
Press on with your plan, because you might
Give yourself, a debt-free life

-Michael "Bart" Mathews

CHAPTER 2
CREDIT MANAGEMENT

*"Today, there are three kinds of people: the
have's, the have-not's,
and the have-not-paid-for-what-they-have's."*

-Earl Wilson

As discussed in chapter one, debt can also cause you major credit problems if you do not pay your bills on time. My once out of control debt caused me to have credit problems. The first thing I did was order a copy of my credit report from all three major credit bureaus; TransUnion, Experian, and Equifax. Next, I took the necessary steps to correct every single credit account on my credit report. I wrote letters and made telephone calls to all three credit bureaus requesting incorrect information be changed or deleted. Read on and discover several other methods that helped me to change my credit situation.

There are several key sources of information that lenders use in determining your credit worthiness. Two sources are your credit report containing your credit history and your credit score. Each source has an impact on your credit.

CREDIT REPORT-DO YOU KNOW WHAT'S IN YOURS?

Every time you borrow money from a creditor or owe money for services, these creditors can report this information to the credit bureaus. This information becomes part of your credit history. It is kept on file with the three major credit reporting agencies, Equifax, Experian, and TransUnion. (See Appendix for credit reporting agency contact information).

Your credit history is used during lending decisions to help determine your credit worthiness, such as; whether you will be approved or denied new or increased credit, the amount of credit, the payback period and the annual percentage rate (APR). The APR determines the total amount of interest you will pay over the repayment period of the loan. Also, some employers use your credit history during hiring decisions.

To put it simply, your credit report is your credit history along with other personal information that has been collected about you. It contains a list of your creditors, the date your credit was opened or closed, your repayment history with number of days late or paid as agreed. Bankruptcy filings, tax liens, and judgments such as auto repossession and foreclosures are also reported.

Your personal information will consist of some of the following, but not limited to:

- Name
- Current address
- Prior addresses
- Place of employment
- Social Security number
- Date of birth
- Telephone numbers
- Names of companies who have requested your credit report (i.e. inquires)

The credit reporting agencies may sell your credit history to businesses in the U.S. and abroad. Credit providers may use this information to send you loan or credit card invitations with offers from zero percent to high interest rates depending on your credit history and credit score. You can elect to opt out and stop the unsolicited credit offers from filling up your mailbox simply by calling the Opt Out toll free number. You can also make a written request to the credit agencies to opt out of solicitations. (See Appendix for Opt Out contact information).

Your credit history is the heartbeat of your financial future. It is critical that you monitor and protect it as you would anything you own of value. The best way to find out what is in your credit report is for you to order a copy from all three credit reporting agencies. A fee could be charged, but if you were recently denied credit, this fee might be waived. Federal law allows you to get a free credit report (not score) every 12 months so you can verify your credit information. The website (www.annualcreditreport.com) was created for this purpose so you have no excuse.

The reason you should obtain a credit report from all the agencies is because the information contained in each file could be different. You need the report from all three bureaus to clean up your credit file.

Have you heard the saying, "Your word is your bond"? Your credit report is an example of your financial bond. If you honored the terms of the agreement with the companies who issued your credit, you could have a good to an excellent credit report. You kept your word and made it your bond because you made your payments on time.

If you failed to honor the terms of the agreement and you were unable to keep your financial word, you could have a poor or bad credit report because you failed to pay on time. Before you make a major purchase such as buying a home, or automobile, wouldn't you like to be prepared to get the lowest interest rate possible? The interest rate you will be awarded is associated with the information in your credit report. The longer you pay your bills on time you stand a better chance of having positive information reported.

Good credit gives you access to a financial world that you can use whenever needed. Just having the peace of mind knowing that you qualify for new credit at a zero or low interest rate is as good as it gets.

CREDIT REPORT ERROR'S - HOW TO FIX THEM?

Inaccurate information listed on your credit report can cause your credit score to be much lower than what it should be. This can happen because of outdated information, incomplete information about you, or worst of all, the information on your credit report is not yours but someone else's.

Here is a common example. You are John Doe Jr., and your father is John Doe Sr., and reside at the exact same address. The credit reporting agencies may incorrectly co-mingle the son's and father's credit information. No one took the time to check the social security numbers or dates of birth. Sometimes the Sr., or Jr., is not listed to help distinguish the father from the son. But the name John Doe remains.

If John Doe Jr., or Sr., never obtains a credit report to check their credit history, this can go undetected for years. Errors in your credit file due to inaccurate information can keep you from getting ahead such as; the job you might be seeking, a checking or savings account, a mobile phone, an apartment or mortgage.

First you can try contacting the creditors who are reporting incorrect information and request them to delete the information that is inaccurate. The longer this type of information remains on your credit report, the lower your credit score might be, which can add up to possible credit rejections and/or higher interest rates.

Once you have a copy of your credit reports and discovered errors, you should immediately contact the credit agencies that provided you with the questionable information and file a dispute. The quickest way to submit the dispute is via the credit reporting agency's website-(see Appendix for credit reporting agency websites). You will be able to view your report and enter the disputed information online. However, you can contact the credit agencies via telephone or mail to file a dispute. You should send in any records (copies only) that can help support the errors you are disputing. The agency will contact the business to help confirm or deny the information.

After the investigation is complete, the agency will send you the results of its findings. If any negative information can't be proven accurate or verified, request that it be deleted. If the negative information remains, have it marked as disputed. Continue to communicate with the credit reporting agencies until the issue is resolved.

After the dispute has been filed and all your follow-up telephone calls and letter writing does not get the information corrected or removed, you have the right to add a statement to your credit file. This statement should include an explanation of the dispute. For example: "This is not my account. It belongs to my spouse." Or "I was ill for X number of months and unable to work."

As you can see, you have the power to clean up your own personal credit report. You could go to a credit repair or consolidation agency, but the "Do It Yourself (DIY)" method is less costly. Remember the goal is to reduce debt, and spending, and to improve your credit history. By going through the DIY process, you will gain valuable information into how the credit reporting agencies function. This process should help you to understand the past credit mistakes that got you into trouble in the first place. Also with your newfound knowledge you can assist a family member or friend in cleaning up their credit file.

WHAT ARE YOUR CREDIT SCORES?

One of the most important things in your credit report is your credit score. Your credit score is used by lenders to determine how much money (credit) to lend you and at what interest rate.

My wife had a conversation with our college sophomore granddaughter. She asked, "Why do companies want to know my credit score?" "What is a credit score?" My wife explained "that your credit score is like your GPA. When students apply for college or jobs, the most effective academic way to distinguish one student from another is usually their GPA. If you have a 3.8 and another applicant has a 2.3, you would most likely get accepted or get the job. The credit score works the same way. For example, if you apply for a job as a bank teller and you have excellent credit, the employer will most likely be willing to give you the job. But if you have a poor credit score, they may be more hesitant. Your credit score is your adult GPA!"

There are two types of credit scores; FICO and VantageScore. Each of the three credit reporting agencies (bureaus) TransUnion, Experian, and Equifax calculate the scores slightly differently. That is one of several reasons why you should always request your credit report and scores from all 3 credit bureaus.

FICO

The more important of the two scores has been the FICO score, created by the Fair Isaac Corporation. FICO scores range from 300 to 850. It is a vital part of your credit health like your blood pressure is to your physical health. Unlike your blood pressure, the higher your credit score, the better your credit health!

FICO scores are used by 90% of lenders. It is a major component of a lender's lending decision-making process. Your FICO score is calculated by each of the three credit bureaus using the information contained in your credit report. The higher the score, the lower the credit risk. Each lender uses your FICO score along with its own strategies and formula to make the final assessment of your creditworthiness or riskiness.

To qualify for the best credit terms, you typically need to fall in at least the 50th percentile as compared to other credit applicants. This translates to a FICO score of 720 or higher. Although, lenders primarily use FICO scores not the percentile ranking to make decisions, your percentile ranking is often provided to you with your score.

To further complicate matters, lenders aren't always looking at the same scores either. Within the FICO category alone, lenders look at thousands of different credit models to assess risk -- but consumers generally only receive a generic FICO score.

The risk is reflected in the interest rate lenders offer to you. The higher your FICO credit score, the lower the interest rate, the lower your FICO score, the higher the interest rate. Therefore, your FICO score can save or cost you many thousands of dollars over your lifetime.

VantageScore

There is another credit score that the bureaus created together in 2006 called the VantageScore. The VantageScore 2.0 range was 501-990. In 2013, VantageScore 3.0 was introduced. The 3.0 ranges are the same as FICO 300 to 850. Both versions are still being used. So why FICO and VantageScore scoring models? Per the website (your. vantagescore.com), the VantageScore provides a score even if you have only one month of credit history and less frequent credit history updates. Credit information can now be made available if you are brand new to credit, those who only use credit occasionally and people who haven't used credit at all recently. Other scoring models require at least six months of credit history and recent credit report updates.

VantageScores are also being used by lenders to make lending decisions. When you add the VantageScore into the mix, this further adds to the confusion in understanding what a "good or excellent" credit score is. It is critical that you know your FICO score and your VantageScore and the difference. Be sure to ask your lender which score(s) from which credit bureau(s) they used to make their decision.

Debt-to-Income Ratio

One other important factor that lenders used during credit decisions is your monthly Debt-to-Income ratio (DTI Ratio = Total Monthly Debt divided by Total Monthly Income). The debt-to-income ratio is a simple but useful measure of your overall finances. The ratio of these two numbers gives the debt-to-income ratio, which indicates how much money is left over for savings, upcoming expenses, and new financial obligations.

The debt ratio is important for individuals to know because a high debt-to-income ratio can indicate future financial problems mainly the inability to pay off new debt. This ratio is also important from the perspective of lenders who avoid loaning to people who have high debt and low income. You should set a goal of having a debt-to-income ratio of below 36 percent. Anything above 36 percent is viewed by lenders as risky. An even better goal is a debt-to-income ratio of below 25 percent, which is considered a good ratio by lenders.

Using the monthly income ($5,500) and debt divided by expense ($4,000) figures from Chapter 2 as an example, your debt ratio would be 73% = ($4,000/$5,500). You will need to reduce your debts and/or increase your income to get a lower ratio before applying for credit.

Your credit score, debt ratio and length of credit along with other information contained in your credit report can, in fact, save or cost you thousands of dollars in interest payments over the years. Your credit score is calculated based on the factors in your credit history such as the amount of debt, repayment history, the number of inquiries and amount of available credit. If you have a bad or low credit score, you may get a very high interest rate. A good to excellent credit score may result in a much lower APR. Remember, the higher the APR, the more interest you pay. One of the best ways to build and maintain a good credit score is by paying your bills on time.

If you are married, you and your spouse both have individual credit scores. However, the credit problems of one spouse could affect your overall credit score when applying for joint credit. You must look at both of your individual credit histories and credit scores when cleaning up your credit. It may be necessary to close joint accounts and/or remove authorized signers (users) from your credit cards to help both spouses improve their credit scores and debt ratios individually.

HOW TO GET CREDIT WITHOUT CREDIT

It is good to learn about credit reports and scores, but if you don't have credit and nobody wants to give you any because you don't have any, what do you do? Doesn't having no credit mean you should be able to get some credit and should have a decent credit score? Unfortunately, no!

Before the recession, it was easy for college students to get a credit card. The card issuers set up a table on college campuses all across America, filling them with credit card applications for the young, financially inexperienced students. Company representatives politely assisted and answered questions during the application process. Knowing that you were not under the supervision of your parents or another responsible adult to help guide you through this critical decision-making process. Some company representatives also sugar coated the important fact that you will have to pay the money back eventually and how much interest would be assessed.

Times have changed, according to a September 2nd, 2015, article in Reuters, millennials are not applying for credit cards by leaps and bounds. They heard credit card horror stories from those students that received the credit cards or from what their parents might have experienced. "The average millennial's credit score is 625, and 28 percent of them are ranked below 579," says NerdWallet, a personal finance website. In the world of credit scores, anything above 660 (out of 850) is considered creditworthy. In today's society, you need a good credit score and credit history to get an apartment, buy a car, obtain a loan, or even to get a job.

Before you consider applying for any credit, you should request a copy of your credit report and credit score. Review the information above for the process to do this and to dispute any information that is incorrect.

If used responsibly, credit cards are a good way to build an excellent credit history. So charge the pizza and use the cash to pay the bill. Charge your books and use the grant or loan money to pay the bill. By the time you graduate, you will have access to a new word of personal financial opportunities because of your excellent credit worthiness during your years on campus. Without a good credit score and credit history, creditors are reluctant to be the first to take a chance on new applicants. So how do you get credit if you don't have any?

One of the best ways to obtain new credit is by using a Secured Credit Card. Basically, these types of cards are secured by you making a small deposit with the card issuer representing the amount of the credit line. The deposit (credit line) amount can range from $300 to $1,000. Make sure you do your research on any fees and limitations to ensure you follow all of the rules. Also, be sure the card issuer will report your payment history to the credit bureau. If not, choose another issuer. Lastly, be sure you make all payments on time and at least the minimum amount due. To ensure you will see a positive credit history and score. See the next section below for more details on secured credit cards.

While it may be possible to get a retail credit card or gas credit card, they often come with an initial low introductory interest rates and then convert to excessively high interest rates after the introductory period. If you go this route, stick with a small credit limit to avoid accumulating an enormous amount of debt.

You must be very careful when selecting or using a credit card to establish your credit history. Be thoughtful and responsible and remember everything you have learned thus far in this book to build and protect your credit history and credit score.

WAYS TO IMPROVE BAD CREDIT

It has been said that a person who fails to plan, plans to fail. If you look at yourself on the outside, you might look like a million dollar bonus baby because of all the fancy material things that you spent your money on. But when your money ran out you used other people's money in the form of credit and you piled up more debt. You now have more debt than income and can no longer pay your bills. Your credit history is at a low point, and the need for bankruptcy protection is on the table for consideration.

If you file for bankruptcy, Chapter 7 or Chapter 13, you will receive some relief from your debts. Chapter 7 will eliminate all of your installment loan debt. Chapter 13 consolidates all of your debt payments into one lower monthly payment for 36 to 60 months. You must maintain a steady income under Chapter 13.

Maybe you decided not to file for bankruptcy and instead dig yourself out of your financial sinkhole on your own. Whatever the case may be, with a plan of action along with financial literacy education you can improve your situation.

Television commercials that advertise get out of debt and credit repair and counseling services are common because so many people have bad credit and are deep in debt. Some of the agencies charge a fee and some offer free help. However, if you take your time and look into your own credit history, you can improve your overall credit profile on your own. If you have poor or bad credit, you have the necessary tools to right most wrongs that you discover. Take time to learn so you can benefit more from the money you earn. Why pay someone else to do what you can learn to do for yourself?

The most effective way to improve your credit situation is to pay your debts on time and to reduce/eliminate debt as quickly as possible. The following three sections will provide you with other options that could help improve or build your credit.

1. Improve Your Credit via Secured Credit Accounts

With a secured credit account, you can start to build new credit or rebuild your credit history. Secured credit accounts can be either a credit card or a loan that is secured (guaranteed) usually in 1 of 2 ways: a savings account or the equity in your home called collateral. If secured by the equity in your home, there are 2 types of loans commonly used called home equity loan or home equity line of credit (HELOC).

To obtain a secured credit card or loan, you go to any financial institution offering these products and inquire about the terms of the agreement that comes along with opening up the account. Next, if you agree to the terms and decide to go forward, you will need to know the dollar amount required by the lending institution as well as any fees associated with doing so.

I suggest you do your research and try to find a no or low fee service provider. After this is completed, you will fill out all necessary paperwork, pay the required fee and deposit the required dollar amount needed to get your secured credit card or loan into a savings account. Usually, the opening amount is around $300 to $1,000 depending on the institution.

Your goal is to build or rebuild your credit to a respectable rating. Now that you have your secured credit card you have another chance to act responsibility with both your finances and your credit. Use the credit card by charging something every billing cycle. It is important to make the minimum payment every billing cycle because your payment history will be reported to the credit reporting agencies every thirty days. The real goal is to completely pay off the balance each month to ensure that you do not accrue any more additional debt! For the example below, you use your card to purchase gasoline for your car during the month.

You are going to spend, let's say $300.00 per month on fuel. Instead of paying cash you now pay at the pump with your secured credit card. I repeated the gas example again because, for those of us who drive, we must purchase gas, so why not find a way to benefit from making this purchase. Maybe you want to set up one of your household bills (telephone or electric) on automatic bill pay to take the worry out of making a purchase every billing cycle.

For the secured loan account, you get a loan based on the amount of the equity you have available in your home or one secured by a savings account. Regardless of type, you will be given the funds up front along with a set monthly payment amount and schedule.

Don't forget what got you in credit despair in the first place. Be sure you never exceed the spending limit on your card and make at least all your required minimum payments on time. Over time, you will see your credit history improve along with your credit score. As this happens, something magical within you takes over your thinking. You are starting to feel better about yourself because you see a positive change as you make financial progress due to your own actions.

As long as you make all your monthly payments on time and you pay the minimum amount due, the financial institution will send the three credit bureaus a positive payment history. These transactions are now a part of your credit history, which will over time help build/rebuild your credit score. These things alone will not give you the type of credit history and score you most desire, but by taking one step at a time you will see improvements. An added bonus is that you can earn interest on the balance of your savings account.

2. The Advantage of using Reward Credit Cards

With so many credit cards, companies are pulling out all the stops trying to lure you into using their card. Make sure the credit card you use has a system that rewards you for using their bank card. But be aware that reward credit cards may come with higher interest rates but if you pay off the balance each month and use it just to build up rewards, you can reap the full benefits.

Examples of rewards:

- cashback
- airline tickets
- car rentals
- hotel rooms
- vacation packages
- dining
- theater
- gas
- pre-loaded gift cards
- and much more

The following example is showing you one way to use your credit card to build rewards. Let's say you spend $300.00 per month on gas and you use cash or a debit card every time you pay. Make this simple change and charge that same $300.00 on your rewards credit card allowing you to build up reward points. The key is that you should set aside the $300.00 in cash and don't spend it until the credit card due date arrives. Then pay off the credit card in full each and every month to avoid interest charges and debt accumulation. By using your rewards based credit card wisely you can realize five key financial benefits:

1. Earn Reward Points.
2. By paying off your balance in full every month, "paid as agreed" will be reported to the credit reporting agencies.
3. Reduce the amount of interest you pay each month to zero.
4. You pay no late fee because you always pay on time.
5. You don't accumulate a large amount of revolving debt.

If you can do this, it could turn out to be the way you can now afford that long awaited trip to anywhere in the world. You can fly first class as well as stay in a five-star hotel all paid for with your airline/hotel reward travel points. My wife and I vacationed in Paris using credit card reward points so I know it works.

WARNING! When using any credit, you must show absolute discipline and never charge more than you can repay in full each and every month! No exceptions, period! Every month you want to start off with a zero balance.

3. Increase Your Income

Are you happy with what you are earning? What income changes can you make that will provide you with more cash to pay down your debt and help improve or start a savings plan and create investment capital? I often hear people say that money is the root of all evil. Could it be that money is not evil, but the lack of financial responsibility with money is evil?

Are you spending your hard earned money on things you don't need, to impress people you don't know? Are you piling up thousands of dollars of debt with high interest rates? Are you living paycheck to paycheck? Do, you have to work overtime or get a second job or move in with your family, your in-laws or maybe a friend to survive? Some people have been reduced to living in a shelter while others have experienced homelessness at one time or another.

That sounds like evil to me. What do you think? Money is just a medium of exchange. There are legal ways to obtain additional income: Two most common methods are earned income and passive income:

- **Earned Income** is income you make when you exchange hours for dollars working a job. Even if your job is paying you twenty thousand, sixty thousand, or one hundred thousand dollars or just making minimum wage, if you go to work every day you are earning your income. So, if you stopped working and had no other source of financial means, how would you maintain your current lifestyle? And for how long?

- **Passive Income** is when your assets are earning you income, like rent from income-producing property or interest or dividends from savings accounts, bonds, stocks, annuities, certificate of deposits and other investments. If you have a passive stream of income that is enough to meet your monthly living expenses, you no longer are required to work. Remember, retirement is based on money, not age. If you have enough monthly passive income regardless of age, would you get up Monday morning, in the middle of January during a bitterly cold Chicago winter and go to work? Wouldn't it be nice to roll over instead of rolling out of bed?

Go ahead and work overtime, get a second job, ask your boss for a raise or move in with your family to increase your income. Consider turning your talents into extra money; baking, doing taxes, weekend daycare service (only if you really like children) and so on. Go back to school and get a degree or learn a trade (e.g. computer repair). Buy rental property. Do whatever it takes to increase your available income.

Once your debts and expenses begin to decrease, your credit score will start to increase along with your positive cash flow. You can begin enjoying the fruits of your labor and take advantage of the actual power of money and chart your course to building wealth.

One additional action you must take to protect your new and improved credit is to proactively monitor your credit report and score on a regular basis. There are credit monitoring services available for a fee through the 3 major credit bureaus as well as other credit monitoring companies. These companies can send you email and/or text messages to notify you of any changes to your credit report. Some companies offer free credit report monitoring–(see Appendix for free credit report resources).

Remember, self-discipline, patience and persistence is the most important pieces of the "get out of debt" management process. If you ever need assistance with how to lower your debt, you can contact the National Foundation For Consumer Credit Counseling services-(see Appendix for contact information). Also, visit my website (www.tmeginc.com) for additional resources to assist you in getting out of debt.

KNOW YOUR CREDIT RIGHTS

Your credit is valuable. The importance of how much credit you have and how you use it goes far beyond shopping. Whether you have excellent, good or poor credit can affect where you live and even where you work, because your credit record may be considered by prospective employers. That is why you need to understand how credit is awarded or denied, what you can do if you are treated unfairly and what agencies are available to assist you and to protect your rights.

Consumer Credit Protection Act – Laws Protecting Consumer Rights

The Consumer Credit Protection Act (CCPA) was created in 1968 to help guarantee American consumers fair and ethical credit practices. This federal legislation standardized practices to ensure that lenders throughout the country followed the same sets of regulations.

As banking and credit reporting evolved, additional laws were developed and put into place under the Consumer Credit Protection Act. Although each act has a different specialty, they share a common trait. They were designed to protect consumers.

The CCPA is the umbrella in which all of the consumer credit related Acts fall under. Below is a list of the central Acts. As a result of the financial and housing crisis started in 2008, these Acts were enhanced to provide further protection. Numerous websites contain details on your rights under each of these acts:

- Fair Credit Reporting Act (FCRA)
- Equal Credit Opportunity Act (EEOC)
- Fair Credit Billing Act
- Truth in Lending Act
- Fair Debt Collection Practices Act
- Electronic Fund Transfer Act

Fair Credit Reporting Act (FCRA)

This act details your credit reporting rights. The United States Congress passed the Fair Credit Reporting Act in 1970. You should obtain a copy of FCRA so you can fully understand your credit reporting rights. (See Appendix for FCRA contact information).

Some of the fundamental rights described in FCRA limits the number of copies of your credit report a company may receive. If the company which obtains your credit report takes adverse action against you, like denying you credit, they must inform you in writing. You are also entitled to get the name of the agency who gave up the adverse information along with a free copy of your credit report. This will allow you to confirm or deny the validity of the report in a timely manner.

You are entitled to a free credit report once a year even if you have not applied for and been denied credit within a twelve month period. The fact remains that there is no problem for you to obtain a copy of your credit report. Your credit report is the heart and soul of maintaining your good financial name, so protect it and keep it clean at all cost.

Consumer Financial Protection Bureau (CFPB)

As a result of the financial and housing crisis that began in 2008, the Consumer Financial Protection Bureau (CFPB) was created in July 2010. It became the country's first federal agency to focus on consumer financial protection. Its creation was part of the Dodd-Frank Wall Street Reform and Consumer Protection Act, which Congress passed to overhaul the country's financial regulations in the wake of the Great Recession.

The CFPB's mission is to protect consumers in regards to financial services and products, as well as to encourage fair practices within consumer financial markets.

The primary responsibilities of the CFPB are to write and enforce laws for financial services companies and products. It has investigative and enforcement authority, with the power to issue subpoenas and request testimony in federal court. The CFPB also is tasked with reviewing and streamlining regulations previously put in place by seven different federal agencies, which shared responsibility for the rulemaking, supervision, and enforcement of consumer financial protection.

The CFPB inherited laws from the following federal agencies:

1. Department of Housing and Urban Development
2. Federal Deposit Insurance Corporation (FDIC)
3. Federal Reserve Board
4. Federal Trade Commission
5. National Credit Union Administration
6. Office of the Comptroller of the Currency
7. Office of Thrift Supervision

The Dodd-Frank Act further requires the CFPB to ensure that consumers have access to information in plain English about their financial options such as mortgages, loans, and credit cards agreements.

The CFPB's Division of Consumer Education and Engagement runs programs and initiatives to educate consumers and empower them to make informed decisions. The Division has programs targeted toward particular populations such as students, members of the armed forces and older Americans. The related Office of Financial Empowerment, launched in June 2012, specifically addresses the needs of low-income and other economically vulnerable Americans.

The CFPB invites consumers to discuss their experiences with financial products and services via a variety of forums such as town hall meetings, logging on to the CFPB's website and field hearings. The CFPB's Office of Community Affairs also invites local leaders to speak at forums regarding consumer and civil rights.

In July 2011, a year after the CFPB was founded, the bureau began its consumer response operations to accept and process direct consumer complaints. Consumers can file complaints through its website and by telephone, mail, fax and email. The CFPB only accepted complaints about credit cards but later began allowing complaints about mortgages, bank services, consumer loans and private student loans.

Avoid Credit Repair Scams

According to the Federal Trade Commission website (www.consumer.ftc.gov), you should be aware of how to spot a credit repair scam. You'll know you're encountering credit repair fraud if a company:

- insists you pay them before they do any work on your behalf
- tells you not to contact the credit reporting companies directly
- tells you to dispute information in your credit report — even if you know it's accurate
- tells you to give false information on your applications for credit or a loan

- doesn't explain your legal rights when they say what they can do for you

You should also avoid ads that promise a "New Credit Identity" or "New Credit File." These companies promising a "new credit identity or file" say they can help you hide bad credit history or bankruptcy for a fee. Their goal is to have you apply for credit using a new nine-digit number called a CPN-credit profile/privacy number. This number is not a substitute for your social security number and could actually be stolen social security numbers resulting in "identity theft".

They may also ask you to apply for an EIN number which is a business tax id issued by the IRS. While the EIN would be legitimate, you are now responsible for a business that you may not be able to pay the fees, licenses, taxes, etc.

If you follow a credit repair company's advice and commit fraud, you might find yourself in legal trouble. It's a federal crime to:

- lie on a credit or loan application
- misrepresent your Social Security number
- obtain an EIN from the IRS under false pretenses

The bottom line is that if you use the number they sell you, you could face fines or time in prison.

The Credit Repair Organization Act (CROA) makes it illegal for credit repair companies to lie about what they can do for you and to charge you before they've performed their services. This law, which is enforced by the Federal Trade Commission, requires credit repair companies to explain:

- your legal rights in a written contract that also details the services they'll perform
- your three-day right to cancel without any charge
- how long it will take to get results
- the total cost you will pay
- any guarantees

What if a credit repair company you hired doesn't live up to its promises? You have the right to sue them in federal court either individually or as part of a class action lawsuit and to seek punitive damages and attorney fees.

IDENTITY THEFT

Last and equally important is to protect yourself against identity theft. The downside of good credit is that someone may want to steal it. Identity theft can destroy your credit and your life. You should take some necessary measures to protect your identity. Some examples are below:

- Invest in a good cross-cut document shredder and shred all documents containing your personal information; account numbers, credit card offers, life insurance offers, etc.
- Never give out your passwords or security codes to anyone.
- Don't use passwords that can be easily known (such as birthdates, addresses and nicknames) and change your passwords often.
- Invest in a safe deposit box at your local bank and store all documents with sensitive information such as passports, birth certificates, wills, trusts, etc.
- Make copies of important documents that you carry with you such as social security number, driver's license number, state ID, and work ID and keep in your safe deposit box as well.
- Never give out your personal information online or by telephone if you did not initiate the communication.
- Monitor your credit reports regularly (Equifax, Experian, and TransUnion). The credit bureaus along with other companies offer credit monitoring services for free or a fee.
- Obtain a P.O Box and use this address on your checks instead of your home address.
- Do not have your social security number printed on your personal checks for the world to see!

If you or someone you know has been a victim of identity theft, the steps below can help assist you in limiting the damage you might incur:

- Cancel your credit cards immediately! By keeping a complete list of all credit card names, card numbers and the toll-free numbers within your reach, at a moment's notice you can make all the necessary calls.
- File a police report in the area (jurisdiction) where your wallet or purse was stolen or lost. By doing this, you now have a legal document on file representing proof of your claim of theft or loss. You also are showing the credit card service providers that your due diligence in stopping the financial bleeding that might happen by this unfortunate event is sincere.
- Call or go online to the three credit reporting agencies (Equifax, Experian, and TransUnion) and request that a fraud alert be added to your credit file. By taking this action, all companies will automatically be on alert of possible identity theft involving your personal information.

Summary

Bottom line, pay your debts on time and protect your financial information! Your credit is a tool, if used wisely, can save you or cost you thousands of dollars during your lifetime based on the interest rate you qualify for. List and photocopy everything that you carry in your purse or wallet. Credit cards, debit cards, driver's license, state identification, work identification, etc., along with accounts numbers, expiration dates, issuing institutions name, address and phone numbers. Keep this information in a safe place where you can reach it ASAP. (See Appendix for Identity Theft resource information). **REMEMBER, "THE BEST IMPROVEMENT STARTS WITH SELF IMPROVEMENT"**

POEM - DON'T DESPAIR

When you buy on credit, and get into debt

Having spent your money, becomes your regret

You lost your home, and now you must rent

You have no idea, of what you have spent

Your new situation you currently hate

Bad credit and debt, all bills are now late

But Don't Despair

There are ways, to help you repair

If you pay on time and cut up your cards

Things won't continue to be so hard

You have no savings, and cannot invest

Your survival is now put to the test

Your financial plan hits an all-time low

And now your retirement dream might go

But Don't Despair

There are ways to help you repair

Reduce your spending, and you should see

Some extra cash, but don't go on, a spending spree

-Michael "Bart" Mathews

CHAPTER 3
KNOW YOUR NET WORTH

*"If you don't know where you are or where you
are going in life financially,
how will you know when you get there and
how much money you will need to stay?"*

–Robbie Mathews

YOUR TOTAL ASSETS minus your total debt/liabilities equal your net worth. Do you know your net worth? Let me ask you a question, Financially Speaking, if you don't know where you are going, how will you know that you have arrived? Look around at all you have accumulated and put a price tag on it. Your net worth includes anything that you own that has financial value along with anything that you owe. How to determine your net worth is discussed in this chapter.

Knowing your net worth is a vital part of your personal planning. Knowing your net worth will give you most of the necessary financial information needed to plan for other areas of your life. I will explore the other planning aspects with you later in the book. But for now, let's keep the focus on knowing your net worth.

In Chapter 1-Debt Management, I suggested that you list all of your debts, also known as liabilities. If you already have your list, you are ready to move to the next step in determining your net worth. If you have not done so, STOP now. Take the necessary time and make your debts/liabilities list. Remember, if you are a couple, it is important for both partners to be completely honest when listing all assets and liabilities.

Now that you have your debt/liabilities list, the next step is to list all of your assets. Examples of assets include but are not limited to:

- investments: stocks, bonds, mutual funds and certificates of deposit
- cash (on hand, in the bank, under the mattress, etc.)
- savings
- retirement accounts: 401k, 457, traditional IRA, Roth IRA
- life insurance
- real-estate (use the current market value not what you paid for the property)
- automobiles
- all other personal property such as furs, jewelry, gold, art, collectibles, etc.

In order to determine your Net Worth, you will need to determine the current market value of each of your assets. The formula for finding your net worth is simply your Total Assets value minus your Total Liability (debts) amount (Net Worth=Total Asset Value - Total Liability Amount).

If your total assets are greater than (>) your liabilities, you will have a "positive" net worth. On the other hand, if your total asset value is less than (<) your total liability (debts) amount, you have a "negative" net worth.

Below is an illustration of an example of a net worth form. It contains sample assets and liabilities showing a positive net worth of $35,700. If you have a positive net worth, you can think about adding a higher payment amount to a creditor to speed up the payment of a debt. You might want to increase your retirement savings contribution by a percent or two. These two things can further increase your net worth and cash flow.

However, if you change the primary mortgage balance in the illustration from $200,000 to $250,000, your net worth would be a negative $-14,300. If you have a negative net worth, re-read the Chapter 1-Debt Management for ways to reduce your debt and liabilities.

You can use this form as a guide to determine your own net worth. Just replace the list of assets and liabilities with the list you created in the Debt Management chapter using steps 1 and 2. Remember when valuing your assets; use the actual purchase price as your starting point. Now list the current market value (which may be higher or lower than the original purchase price). This will allow you to see if your assets increase in value or depreciated in value. Also, the internet is a good source for net worth calculators and forms to help you with this task.

TABLE 3.1 - NET WORTH CALCULATION SAMPLE

Sample Net Worth Form

Your net worth as of Month, YYYY

ASSETS		LIABILITIES	
Cash		**Long Term**	
Checking	$1,500	**Primary Mortgage**	$200,000
Savings	$1,000	Second Mortgage	
Certificates of Deposit		Equity Credit Loan	
Money Market		Other	
Credit Union Savings	$500	Total Long-Term Debt	$200,000
Other savings		**Short Term**	
Total Cash	$3,000	Auto Loan	$20,000
Fixed Term		Credit Cards	$15,000
US Savings Bonds	$200	Student Loans	$30,000
Municipal Bonds		Other Loans	
Corporate Bonds		Total Short-Term Debt	$265,000
Bond Mutual Funds		**Total Liabilities**	**$330,000**
Total Fixed	$200		
Equity			
Stocks			
Stock Mutual Funds	$5,000		
Rental Real Estate			
Investment Real Estate			
Retirement Plans (e.g. 401k)	$5,000		
Total Equity	$10,000		
Business			
Estimated Value			
Personal			
Primary Residence	$325,000		
Vacation Homes			
Autos	$25,000		
Jewelry	$2,500		
Furs			
Antiques			
Other			
Total Personal	$352,500		
Total Assets	**$365,700**	**Positive Net Worth**	**$35,700**
If you change your ** Primary Mortgage Liability to $250,000 your Net Worth would become negative:**		**Negative Net Worth**	**-$14,300**

Summary

Knowing your net worth is an important factor in your financial planning. Your net worth number will determine if you are on the right track for retirement. Also, what changes you should consider in your financial planning that can add additional security for you and your family. Do not be a wandering generality. Be a meaningful specific. Calculate your net worth to get a realistic picture.

It's never too late to start changing some things in your life. The earlier you start taking your personal financial health seriously today, the better off your financial outcome should be tomorrow and beyond!

REMEMBER, "THE BEST IMPROVEMENT STARTS WITH SELF IMPROVEMENT."

POEM - STAY THE COURSE

When you start on the road to success

You must really try hard and do your best

Life`s challenges are always a test

If you want to succeed, you have no time to rest

The crabs in the barrel try to pull you down

Keep a sharp look out, they're all around

Stay one step ahead, and never look back

March on to victory you're on the right track!

-MICHAEL "BART" MATHEWS

CHAPTER 4
BUILDING WEALTH: CREATE A LEGACY

"Tell me and I forget. Teach me, and I may remember. Involve me, and I learn."

-Benjamin Franklin

A T THIS POINT in the book, you should begin to believe it is possible to gain control of your financial future if you are really serious about it. You have read about ways to lower, then eliminate your debt, generate positive cash flow, how to clean up your credit history, improve your credit score, and determine your net worth. Let us continue the journey and look at some principles of wealth building. I will reveal the actual secret to success!

What is Wealth Building? Wealth building is an accumulation of assets that provide current and future generations with sustainable streams of income if managed correctly. To build wealth, you need strategies that will allow you to accumulate, grow, protect and distribute your money during and after your lifetime.

There was no discussion of wealth-building concepts in my house when I was growing up. My father's idea of financial security was getting up every day going to work day in and day out just to get a pension and social security at age 65. Business ownership was never discussed even though my mother had a home based business in addition to working a job. I think she did it for extra income, not to build wealth.

No one has the same definition of wealth. You need to define it for you and your family and determine how wealthy you want to become. How much wealth you accumulate depends on your knowledge of wealth-building principles and how you apply them.

WHAT IS REAL WEALTH?

King Solomon, the son of King David, was wealthy in his own right. He was full of knowledge and wisdom as well as material possessions. Solomon is known for his vast amount of knowledge and wisdom during critical times in history. The King Solomon's of today are Bill Gates (Microsoft), Warren Buffett (Berkshire Hathaway), Larry Ellison (Oracle), and Oprah Winfrey (OWN) among many others. This list goes on and on. They all have something in common with King Solomon; they all accumulated vast amounts of legacy wealth along with acquiring knowledge while helping current and future generations (philanthropy).

Do you believe that the rich get richer, and the poor get poorer? What makes one person wealthy, while others are not? Acquiring knowledge of wealth building principles, plus taking action is one way the rich get richer. Building wealth really has no real secrets, but the wealthy follow proven wealth building principles that have withstood the test of time. Wealthy people gained the necessary knowledge and put it into actual use. And so can you!

On March 2nd, 2015 Forbes 29th annual list of world billionaires were featured. There were 1,826 billionaires worldwide. Holding down the top position on the list is American Bill Gates, the number one richest person in the world at $ 79.2 billion. The second position is held by Mexico's Carlos Slim Helu with $77.1 billion. The third richest person in the world is American Warren Buffett with $72.7 billion. The fourth position is held by Spain's Amanico Ortega with 64.5 billion and American Larry Ellison rounding out the top five wealthiest people in the world comes in fifth with $54.3 billion.

290 new billionaires made the 2015 list representing the world's richest. The list of the world's wealthiest is constantly changing and growing. In chapter six you will read that Bill and Melinda Gates and Warren Buffett both pledged to give away a vast amount of wealth to charitable organizations while enlisting pledges from other billionaires to do likewise. That's a great example of capitalism with a consciousness!

I mention this list of global billionaires because they are living proof of Napoleon Hill's statement, "Whatever the mind can conceive and believe, it can achieve."

Maybe becoming a billionaire is not something that you can imagine at this moment but you can improve your financial situation. My point is, "you do have a choice" and the choice is yours to make! You can work a job and save. You can invest part of your earned income. You can become an entrepreneur and start your own business, either the old fashioned brick and mortar or home based or you can partner up with an existing business. There are many choices you can make to begin to create and build wealth.

Have you ever heard that the word JOB means" Just Over Broke" Don't get me wrong, I would rather be employed or own my own business than be unemployed. But what would you do with no job and no income? How would you live? Who would you ask for help?

Why do you think so many people play the Powerball and the Mega Millions lottery? Why do people go to the casino or the riverboat to gamble? Because they want the chance to capture the pot of gold at the end of the rainbow called wealth. Unfortunately, many instant lottery millionaires go broke between five and seven years. Why, because the lack of financial literacy, not knowing how to invest, protect and preserve that new found windfall. Not to mention all of the long-lost relatives and friends that suddenly appear out of the woodwork. For some, winning the lottery could be a blessing or a curse.

Some people follow basic wealth building principles like saving and investing in interest-bearing accounts over time to accumulate vast amounts of wealth. That was more lucrative back in the day when financial institutions were paying double-digit interest rates on those types of accounts. Today, in 2015 those same accounts pay less than one percent interest yielding a minimal financial return for parking your hard earned cash in a checking, savings or certificate of deposit account. While others have no saving or investing habits and never followed any kind of wealth building principles.

Just for the record, wealth is not all about money. There is spiritual, physical, mental, intellectual, marital, and service wealth factors that one can benefit from. Let's be honest right here, right now. Money is critical to your survival. We all need air to breath and money to feed! *Zig Ziglar said, "Money isn`t the most important thing in life, but it`s reasonably close to oxygen on the "gotta have it" scale."* Try living without one or the other in today`s society. Just don't lose sight of the other vital elements of humanity.

What if you had enough wealth that allowed you to help the less fortunate in some way or another while you attained everything that you needed and wanted? However, if you did have enough wealth, would you continue doing the same thing that you are doing today? Or would you practice sound financial accumulation and preservation principles?

Our goal is to build a legacy by generating a significant amount of wealth and financial knowledge to be passed on to our children, grandchildren, great-grandchildren and future generations thereafter. We also participate in charitable programs allowing others to benefit in some way, shape, form or fashion from a portion of what we have been blessed to acquire.

The following sections and chapters will provide details on various wealth-building strategies:

- Saving – interest bearing checking, savings, Certificate of Deposits (temporary places to park your money

during your personal financial literacy education journey)
- Investing – stocks, bonds, mutual funds, etc.
- Real Estate Investing – personal and income producing
- Entrepreneurship – start you own business/partner up with existing business
- Philanthropy – giving back
- Planning – financial, retirement, tax, insurance, health, estate
- Legacy – creating and substaining generational wealth

SAVING

"If you save as much money in the next five years equal to the amount you saved in the past five years, how much money would you have?"

–MICHAEL BART MATHEWS

I will start with saving because it is the simplest and basic starting point when you have a positive cash flow. How many people do you know are living paycheck to paycheck and do not have any kind of savings plan in place what so ever?

The easiest way to begin accumulating wealth is by saving money in a savings account. The key is to pay yourself first because you will need cash to invest. I need to explain this further. Paying yourself first doesn't mean going out and buying new shoes each payday and wearing your money on your feet. It means that you take out a certain amount of money from each paycheck and put it into a savings account (later to be used for investing) before paying anyone else. You can do this until you gain the necessary knowledge to invest in more aggressive financial vehicles.

The general rule is to save at least 10%-20% of all you earn every time you get paid. The higher the percentage, the more available investment capital you will accumulate over time. You should arrange for your savings to be automatically deducted from your paycheck and deposited directly into an interest bearing account.

Another method of savings is the 52-week Savings Plan. I was speaking with a good friend, Fred Marberry (he turned 80-years-young in 2015). He brought this concept to my attention while sharing some of his old school knowledge and wisdom. Typically you would start this plan the first week in January but you can start at any point in the year and proceed for 52 weeks. Below is a sample of how your savings would grow over the 52-week period.

Basically, you save the dollar amount associated with the week number and mark off the week. The first week you start you save $1.00. The second week you save $2.00, and you will have a $3.00 balance, the third week you save $3.00 ending up with a $6.00 balance. By the 40th week, you will save $40.00 and have an overall balance of $820.00. Now just continue until completion of the entire 52 week saving goal has been reached.

Table 4.1 52 Week Savings Plan

52 Week Saving Plan Sample					
Week	Deposit	Balance	Week	Deposit	Balance
1	$ 1.00	$ 1.00	27	$ 27.00	$ 378.00
2	$ 2.00	$ 3.00	28	$ 28.00	$ 406.00
3	$ 3.00	$ 6.00	29	$ 29.00	$ 435.00
4	$ 4.00	$ 10.00	30	$ 30.00	$ 465.00
5	$ 5.00	$ 15.00	31	$ 31.00	$ 496.00
6	$ 6.00	$ 21.00	32	$ 32.00	$ 528.00
7	$ 7.00	$ 28.00	33	$ 33.00	$ 561.00
8	$ 8.00	$ 36.00	34	$ 34.00	$ 595.00
9	$ 9.00	$ 45.00	35	$ 35.00	$ 630.00
10	$ 10.00	$ 55.00	36	$ 36.00	$ 666.00
11	$ 11.00	$ 66.00	37	$ 37.00	$ 703.00
12	$ 12.00	$ 78.00	38	$ 38.00	$ 741.00
13	$ 13.00	$ 91.00	39	$ 39.00	$ 780.00
14	$ 14.00	$ 105.00	40	$ 40.00	$ 820.00
15	$ 15.00	$ 120.00	41	$ 41.00	$ 861.00
16	$ 16.00	$ 136.00	42	$ 42.00	$ 903.00
17	$ 17.00	$ 153.00	43	$ 43.00	$ 946.00
18	$ 18.00	$ 171.00	44	$ 44.00	$ 990.00
19	$ 19.00	$ 190.00	45	$ 45.00	$ 1,035.00
20	$ 20.00	$ 210.00	46	$ 46.00	$ 1,081.00
21	$ 21.00	$ 231.00	47	$ 47.00	$ 1,128.00
22	$ 22.00	$ 253.00	48	$ 48.00	$ 1,176.00
23	$ 23.00	$ 276.00	49	$ 49.00	$ 1,225.00
24	$ 24.00	$ 300.00	50	$ 50.00	$ 1,275.00
25	$ 25.00	$ 325.00	51	$ 51.00	$ 1,326.00
26	$ 26.00	$ 351.00	52	$ 52.00	$ 1,378.00

I could not find the original creator of this concept. I found numerous examples of Table 4.1 52-Week Savings Plan illustrated above via a Google internet search. There were also many creative variations on how to achieve the $1,378 (excluding interest) at the end of the 52 weeks. The results below show how your money will grow from year one to year thirty if you follow the plan each year:

- $1,378 savings amount after year one
- $6,890 savings amount after year five
- $13,780 savings amount after year ten
- $20,670 savings amount after year fifteen
- $27,560 savings amount after year twenty
- $34,450 savings amount after year twenty-five
- $41,340 savings amount after year thirty

The above amounts are principal savings only and do not reflect any earned interest payments. If you can afford it, you may want to consider doubling or tripling the weekly amounts to accumulate more savings faster.

Think about it. How many people do you know that have little or no savings and are the exact same age as you? The 52-week Savings Plan is not a substitute for other savings options. It is an additional way of saving a little bit of money at a time. With your new found savings, other investment opportunities can also be seriously considered! Now, there will be one less person without savings.

Your savings account deposits will earn some interest (in 2015 most banks are paying less than one percent interest) depending on the terms. Reinvesting the earned interest (regardless of how little) along with regular deposits allows you to take advantage of the miracle of compounding. Compounding will cause your nest egg to grow faster.

Certificates of deposits do pay a slightly higher rate of interest than regular interest bearing accounts. They have different kinds of interest earning plans that will be offered to you at the time of opening. The terms vary and can include a fixed or variable rate of interest for a fixed period of time.

Some even offer a set amount of penalty-free withdrawals. Again always reinvest all earned interest for faster growth.

Credit unions may be an alternative other than banks. Do your research because both institutions offer low interest rates. You want to choose the one that gives you the most bang for your buck. So do your research and compare.

All are considered safe investments because if you bank at an institution that is a member of the Federal Deposit Insurance Corporation (FDIC), these accounts are all insured up to a certain amount. Check with the financial institution to confirm their membership in the FDIC.

The moral of the story is, just start saving on a regular basis, NOW! Stick to it. No matter how little it might seem today, it can grow into investment capital for the future.

INVESTING

Investing is fundamentally different from saving because of the increased risk of possible loss of principal investment funds. Financial instruments such as stocks, bonds, mutual funds, and real estate, starting a brick and mortar business may not be protected by the FDIC. In other words, you could lose all your capital (the shirt off your back) if your investments turn out not to be good ones. But the advantage of investing versus savings is investing offers you the chance to build wealth at a faster pace because the rate of return (ROI) from investments is usually far higher than with savings. The saying "No Risk, No Reward" is the epitome of the pros and cons of saving versus investing.

Some of the most common types of financial investments are stocks, bonds, and mutual funds. Here is a brief description of these investment instruments:

- **Stocks**: You purchase stock in a company for a certain amount of money. You now own a share or shares depending on the quantity of purchase. You actually own a percentage of the company and in some cases, you are allowed to vote because you are a shareholder. The general rule is to buy low and to sell high. There are **two primary ways for you to profit from stock:**

o **Dividends** is cash paid to shareholders by the company. For example, if you own ten shares of stock and the company pays ten cents per share, you will earn $1.00 in dividends (.10 (cents) times 10 shares). You can choose to reinvest the $1.00 and purchase more stock or take the $1.00 in cash profit. You can have all dividends automatically deposited into your interest bearing account or reinvested into more shares to further aid in the growth of your wealth.

o **Stock Appreciation** occurs when the price of the stock increases. For example, you purchase ten shares of stock for $10.00 a share, for a total value of $100.00. Then the price per share increases by $2.00, or $12.00 per share. The total value of your shares is now worth $120.00 (10 shares times $12). If you sell at $12.00 per share, you will realize a "capital gain" of $20.00 from your initial investment of $100.00, which is a $20.00 profit. The term "unrealized gain" means that you still have a value of $120 because you did not sell the shares to take the profit.

o **Stock Depreciation** occurs when the price of the stock decreases. For example, you purchase ten shares of stock for $10.00 a share, for a total value of $100.00. Then the price per share decreases by $2.00, or $8.00 per share. The total value of your shares is now worth $80.00 (10 shares times $8.00). If you sell at $8.00 per share, you will realize a "capital loss" of $20.00 from your initial investment of $100.00. The term "unrealized loss" means that you still have a value of $80 because you did not sell the shares to take the loss.

• **Bonds** are parts of the family known as fixed income securities. These securities are called debt obligations. In other words, a corporation or government is borrowing money from you. In return, you are paid back the principal plus interest after the maturity period. The maturity period could be short term (e.g. 1-2 years) or long term (e.g. 5+ years).

- **Mutual Funds** are collections of stocks and/or bonds. By investing in mutual funds, you will have a mixture of investments vehicles to help diversify your chances of building wealth. Mutual Funds come in a vast assortment of investment types and categories (e.g. Large Cap Stocks, Small Cap Stocks, Municipal Bonds, Tax Exempt Bonds, Energy Stocks, Green Companies, etc.).

Investing does have some risks as mentioned earlier, but the reward can be well worth the risk. Be careful and do your due diligence through research and/or speak with a certified licensed financial specialist before investing.

Investment Club-What Is It?

One way to possibility minimize the initial fear of investing is to form an Investment Club. Several years ago, my wife and I along with a group of friends and family got together and decided we were going to increase our financial literacy and learn more about investing. We started the "Blessed to Invest" Investment Club. This allowed us to pool our cash contributions together to maximize our capital.

We joined the National Association of Investors Corporation (NAIC) and followed their principles and guidelines for investing and research. The club established bylaws, officers, monthly meetings, and study sessions. We thoroughly researched different stocks to help determine the best possible investment options. The most important thing to me about being an investment club member was having access to the wide variety of educational investment financial tools and resources.

The traditional investment club is formed by a group of members or partners who share the same goals of building wealth through investing in the stock market. There are other groups who not only invest in the stock market, but they also invest in other financial instruments, like real estate, business start-ups, private equity, etc. For this example, I will focus on the traditional investment club investing in the stock market.

The objective is to contribute an equal amount of investment dollars on a consistent, predetermined schedule. The club will purchase stocks on a regular basis after careful, in-depth due diligence from financial literacy research, regardless of whether the stock market is a bull (high) or bear (low). This is the key to taking advantage of the dollar cost averaging principle of investing. The dollar cost averaging principle means you buy more shares when prices are low (bear market) and fewer shares when prices are high (bull market). This helps to minimize any potential losses in value over the long term.

All decisions in the club are made by the power of the members' votes, with the majority rule. This will enable each partner to be heard and each idea will be voted on. The philosophy of the traditional investment club is to stay in for the long haul. And with the understanding it may take several years for the club's investments to yield the expected rate of return.

By establishing an investment club, you can actually reap the benefits of what I call the three OP's which are; Other People's Money, Other People's Time and Other People's Experience. You all will have a much larger principal amount to invest as a group rather than investing alone. Using other people's money to invest is a much better idea than using other people's money to acquire debt (i.e. loans, credit cards). Get the picture? I think you do.

The stock market historically has consistently displayed its resilience resulting in unprecedented growth and profitability despite the numerous times of economic turmoil. Due to the financial crisis that started in 2008, the Dow Jones Industrial Average dropped from approx. 13,000 in April 2008 to 6,600 (bear market) in March 2009.

By December 2013, the Dow Jones was continuing to rebound and reached another all-time high by closing over the 16,500 mark for the first time in history. By September, 2nd, 2014, the Dow was over the 17,000 mark giving the appearance of a climbing bull market, though the economy's future was still uncertain at best. According to a March 28th, 2013 article on Yahoo Finance, it quotes James Altucher as predicting "we could see the Dow reach 20,000 in 2014 or early 2015." His prediction may be slightly off as the Dow only reached 18,054 in December 2014 but dropped back into the 17,000s into early 2015 before bouncing back to the 18,000 levels.

Because of the unpredictable market volatility, on August 24th, 2015, after the sound of the opening bell on Wall Street, the stock market dropped some 1,000 points. At the sound of the closing bell, the DJIA one day point loss was 588, closing at 15,871 points, after experiencing a historic day of market fluctuation. Some investors saw a sell market, others saw a buy market while others decided to hold knowing they could not time the rising Bull or the falling Bear market swings.

How high or low will the stock market go? In reality no one really knows. By the time this book is published, it is possible the Dow Jones will have once again close at a record-setting all-time high as predicted or lower. You can find the Dow Jones Industrial Historical Averages via the website (quotes.wsj.com/DJIA/index-historical-prices).

The stock price is not the only determining factor in selecting stocks. The price to earnings ratio (PE) of stocks has withstood the test of time over the years and is also used in determining the value of a given stock. According to the Intelligent Investor by Benjamin Graham who was Warren Buffet's mentor, when it comes to valuing stocks, the price/earnings ratio is one of the oldest and most frequently used metrics. However, this is not the only metric that should be relied on.

Since the traditional investment club picks stocks to invest in based largely on their average rate of return, the stock market can yield a profit if you invest from a long-term perspective. Stocks are easy to buy and sell, you can invest in some of the most renowned companies in the world. But it is your personal responsibility to know and understand what you are investing in, to obtain the best rate of return (ROI) from your investment dollars. Through research and applied knowledge, you can gain if you are a member of a good investment club, you will be able to establish your investment plan of action to help ensure maximum results.

Starting an Investment Club

Find individuals whom you trust and who share your passion for improving their financial future. Seek members who are willing to invest and pool together money, do research, attend and participate in constructive mastermind meetings. Choose members who are willing to read and educate themselves on how to invest in stocks.

Investment club members can be your neighbors, co-workers, church members, family, and friends who will commit to an "all for one" principle of investing. Here are short guidelines for starting an investment club:

- Set a limit on the number of members-usually 2 to 15. The members will share research assignments as well as hosting meetings. You can also set up a virtual investment club conducting meetings via teleconference calls and/or live streaming video. The positive is it will offer an alternative to hosting monthly meeting in members' homes. The negative is it also takes away the face to face camaraderie and physical interaction needed to gain and maintain trust among members. Tip: Having an odd number of members helps during voting to prevent ties.
- Select club officers at the first meeting: president, vice president, recording secretary, treasurer, and assistant treasurer (I held this position in the Blessed to Invest Investment Club). Each role will have its own set of responsibilities.
- Select a name for the investment club.
- Set meeting dates, times and locations (or rotating locations) among the club members well in advance. Have backup plans for inclement weather.
- Determine the amount of the monthly contributions that must be made by each club member for investing.
- Create the general partnership agreement and bylaws (especially how long the club will exist and the rules for club member withdrawals or drop-outs). Be sure all members sign the agreement and receive their own copy.

- Each club member must file taxes each year with the IRS for their portion of the club's profits or losses.
- Obtain a federal tax identification number for the investment club from the IRS for tax filing purposes. The treasurer usually handles all of the financial arrangements.
- Open a checking account in the name of the investment club. This account will be used for club business only.
- Open a brokerage account, where investment club dues are transferred from the club checking account, to execute stock purchase transactions. Our investment club used a discount brokerage company named Scottrade, which had a lower cost than using a full-service broker. Other discount brokerage companies include but are not limited to Charles Schwab, Ameritrade, and E-Trade. Research all brokerage companies thoroughly before you choose one.

National Association of Investor Corporation (NAIC)

Your club should consider becoming a member of the NAIC. However, you don't have to be a member of an investment club to join the NAIC and take advantage of the wide range of educational tools that they offer.

The four core principles recommended by the NAIC are:

1. Invest regularly regardless of the highs and lows of the market known as dollar cost averaging.
2. Reinvest all earnings.
3. Invest in growth companies.
4. Diversify to reduce your risk.

Before the club votes on what stock or stocks to purchase, NAIC recommends that the NAIC Stock Selection Guide (SSG) be completed. The SSG includes the past history of the stocks' performances as well as future projections as to how well the stocks might perform. With this method of stock selection and education, when the club makes its purchase, it will be based on valuable educated member research.

Investment clubs want to own quality companies that have high growth potential for their investment dollars. You should always monitor your portfolio and continue to buy or sell based on the research and the vote of all members. (See Appendix for NAIC contact information).

This is where my investing mindset switched on and my light bulb really started to shine. Because of doing stock research, I was clearly able to learn and see one of the wealth building principles that millionaires and billionaires have been using for many years. I was never the same again. Parking my cash in a less than one percent bank account was no longer our only investment option. Investing in stocks became part of our new normal. Our stock and other investments over time have outperformed our interest-bearing bank accounts (checking, savings and CDs) by unprecedented numbers thus helping to build our wealth legacy.

OTHER INVESTMENT OPTIONS

- Employer-sponsored benefits plan like a 401k or 457 plan allows you to automatically invest part of your salary for retirement. If you contribute using before-tax dollars, your taxable income will also be reduced. Some companies offer matching contributions. Be sure to invest up to the required percentage to receive matching funds from the company. Don't pass up free money!
- SEP, IRA, and KEOGH are retirement accounts for small business owners and the self-employed. If you are a business owner, consider setting one of these up for yourself and your employees as part of your benefits package.
- Become an entrepreneur. Think outside of the box. Find your passion and make it happen. See Chapter 6-Building Wealth-Entrepreneurship.
- Become a real estate investor. See Chapter 5-Building Wealth-Real Estate Investing.

You may already have a list of your own ways to build wealth, but if you don't, reread this chapter and do your research. I am not giving you investment advice. What I am giving you is a starting point for you to develop your own personal wealth building vision. Everyone wants that pie in the sky or that pot of gold at the end of the rainbow, but what are you willing to learn and do to reach it? If you think you can, you can. If you think you can't, you can't. Either way you are right. What do you think! In order to have what other`s don`t, you must be willing to do what other`s won`t!

Summary

Financially Speaking, the main wealth building key is for you to change the way you think, act and feel about wealth accumulation. Develop a positive mental attitude about becoming wealthy while leaving a legacy for your family while helping others.

Now is the time to find a way to start saving and investing regularly to accumulate wealth. This can be accomplished through automatic payroll deductions or automatic withdrawals from your checking or savings accounts deposited directly into the investment vehicle of your choice.

To build wealth over time and reduce your chances of loss of investment, one must have acquired financial knowledge and understanding. I once believed that if an investment looked too good to be true, it was, because I lacked the sufficient amount of investment knowledge allowing me to be prepared for investment opportunities. I changed my way of thinking and became a student of financial literacy. I researched the many different wealth building principles and investment opportunities that are available.

As promised, the secret to financial success is **YOU** taking action! If you need help, seek out a certified financial professional of your choice. You will be well on your way to building your wealth legacy and changing your Financial DNA For Life!
REMEMBER, "THE BEST IMPROVEMENT STARTS WITH SELF IMPROVEMENT"

POEM - LEAVE A LEGACY

Some are blessed inheriting from birth

Assets minus liabilities equal net worth

Pay off your debts until you have none

Use positive cash flow for your focus fund

Emergency expenses set aside in cash

Use an account to hold this stash

Using positive cash from your balance sheet

Start building wealth without retreat

Diversifying your portfolio some will advise

Asset allocation helps avoid slow growth surprise

Buy low, sell high is one rule of thumb

Learn this trade well and wealth will come

You can't time the markets, as some try to do

Investing in private equity might be for you

When you invest, there are some risks

Wade in shallow waters or swim with the big fish

While building wealth, this is a must

Create a will and a living trust

If you pass on from this life, without written instruction

Your hard earn legacy might fall to destruction

-Michael "Bart" Mathews

CHAPTER 5
BUILDING WEALTH: REAL ESTATE INVESTING

"The single most powerful asset is our mind. If it is trained well, it can create enormous wealth in what seems to be an instant."

-ROBERT KIYOSAKI

HOME OWNERSHIP VS. RENTING

Renting

MY FIRST MEMORIES about renting were when I was around the age of six or seven years old. My parents rented a second-floor apartment from my aunt. My aunt owned a two-flat building with a basement and a two-car garage. She and my cousins lived on the first floor. My parents paid my aunt rent while my aunt paid a mortgage. For each monthly rent payment, my family got to live for another month. But with every monthly mortgage payment my aunt was getting closer to owning the two-flat while building up equity from which she could borrow.

When it came time for my parents to purchase their first single family home they could not use any of the rent money they paid my aunt for a down payment. They had to come up with additional money. When it came time for my aunt to purchase her new single family home, she sold her two flat income producing property and used some of the profits from the sale for the down payment.

As you can see, renters get only what they pay for, one more month to rent. While some property owners get a regular stream of passive income along with the potential for increased equity in their property. If the tenant's rent is enough to pay the mortgage on the property, the property owners can live rent free as well.

Home Ownership

A home is actually a liability as long as it is owned by the lender. However, the debt (mortgage) for a home could be considered good debt because you might one day own-your home free and clear (excluding taxes). Also, in most cases, the interest you pay on your mortgage or equity loan is a tax write off, where the interest you pay on a credit card is not.

As you pay down your mortgage, you begin to establish equity. Equity is the difference between the outstanding principal balance of your mortgage and market value of your home. The equity is actually the percent of the home that you own and can be considered an asset. You can also borrow part or all of the equity value.

For example, the market value of your home is $500,000 and the outstanding principal balance is $250,000. You have $250,000 in equity (borrowing power) or a 50% ownership interest in the home. Once you pay off the mortgage, your home becomes an asset. You must continue to pay for the general upkeep, local real estate taxes, and property insurance premium payment.

Even though there are many benefits to owning your single family home, it does not produce income (unless you rent out a portion of your home) to help pay the associated expenses and liabilities. This means the homeowner must pay the mortgage, taxes, water bill, insurance (including PMI), lawn care, snow removal, alarm system, or general upkeep. Be sure to factor these costs into your home buying decision. You need to be able to afford these home-related expenses as well as food, clothing, child care, transportation, etc., on a monthly basis.

Despite the expenses and liability, homeownership is considered part of the American Dream. Even though there are larger personal responsibilities with home ownership than with renting, home ownership is still for most people a better alternative than renting.

Consider if you were a renter who paid $1,000 per month for 30 years for a total of $300,000 to a two flat building owner who paid $200,000 for the property. After, 30 years you have nothing to show for this money and you would have paid for the property owner's building in full along with giving him/her a $100,000 profit.

If you were paying that same $1,000 per month as the property owner of the 30-yr mortgage, you would own the home after 20 years free and clear (minus taxes and upkeep). You get to keep that $100,000 in your pocket. Not to mention the potential capital gain in value of the property, if you sold it. These are the reasons why property owners have truly benefitted from the American Dream of homeownership and real estate investing.

Homeowner – How Do I Become One?

If you want to become a homeowner, you have to get a mortgage or pay cash. Of course, you can inherit property, use tax liens or auctions but that is not for this discussion. To get a mortgage with the lowest interest rate possible, the first steps in the process are:

1. reduce your debts/expenses
2. clean up your credit history
3. improve your credit score
4. decrease your debt-to-income ratio.

Please review the preceding chapters for this information.

Next, you can begin researching mortgage rates and the price of homes in the area where you want to purchase. The internet has a multitude of sources and information on all types of properties (e.g. single family, condo, townhome, etc.) available for sale. These sources contain all details of the properties such as square footage, price, schools nearby, property taxes, purchase type (e.g. lender, foreclosure, short sale, by owner), agents, etc. There is also a variety of "real estate apps" available to download on your electronic devices to assist with your search.

The next important step in the process is to get pre-qualified. You can get pre-qualified over the telephone, by filling out an application online, or by scheduling an appointment with a loan officer for a more personal session. During this process, the following information will be verified:

- information in the application
- income and employment verification
- asset review
- proof of funds
- credit check (would be done during pre-qualification)
- down payment amount and source of funds
- LTV-Loan to Value Ratio – requested mortgage amount (minus the down payment) divided by value of property – lenders generally like this ratio to be less than 80 percent

Once you complete the pre-qualification steps, and you are approved, a set amount of money that you can use for the purchase of your property will be established. Depending on how good your credit is and your debt-to-income ratio, you could possibility get a no down payment or a low down payment loan. Some lending institutions will offer no closing costs as well or are willing to negotiate the closing cost with you.

Once you receive your pre-qualified approval from your lending institution, this shows the real estate agents and the property sellers that you're serious and are ready to make an offer if the right deal presents itself. It could also give you a better edge when it comes time to negotiate the price.

Once you make an offer on the property and it is accepted, the mortgage loan process begins. During the mortgage loan process, you will need to choose a loan that's right for you. There are many different mortgage loan options available; however, the most common ones are:

- **Conventional** – the majority of these types of loans are 30-year terms. You can get a 15-, 20- or 25-year term, but the monthly payments for these tend to be higher. The shorter the term, the less you pay in interest over the life of the loan.
- **Adjustable Rate Mortgage (ARM)** – these loans are tied to some type of financial index such as the prime rate. The rate is increased or decreased depending upon the index. The period between adjustments can range from months to years. As the rate changes so do your monthly mortgage payments, usually causing your current payment to increase if the index rate increases. However, the payment will be lower if the index rate decreases. You must be careful with these loans and ensure there is some sort of adjustment cap or limit is placed on rate increases. Otherwise, your monthly payment may balloon higher and become unaffordable, like sub-prime mortgage loans that contributed to the foreclosures crisis across America that started in 2008.

Regardless of the type of mortgage loan you select, try not to agree on any kind of prepayment penalty associated with obtaining a mortgage. You do not want to be charged a fee just in case you are able to pay your mortgage off early. Also, be sure to get Truth In Lending and HUD-1 closing statements from the lender with preliminary estimates of the cost to purchase your property. The final version will be presented at closing.

Paying Cash - If you are a cash buyer, you have more negotiation power because cash is king. You also have a much larger inventory of property to choose from because of the economic climate of today's' housing market. Most agents will require a proof of funds letter from your financial institution to ensure that you are a financially qualified buyer. You will be able to purchase distressed properties below market value quicker with cash. A good deal of sweat equity and a lot of patience will be needed during the rehab phase to turn this property from an eyesore, into the dream property of a potential buyer.

You can also negotiate and purchase turn-key properties under market value with cash. And you will have no mortgage payments with a cash deal. What you will have is a 100 percent equity asset. Cash buyers avoid most but not all of the issues that people who finance property must deal with. Remember cash is king!

The final step is the closing process for cash and mortgage buyers. Both will receive a final detailed HUD-1 closing statement. It will contain all costs associated with the sale. The costs can include but are not limited to:

- appraisal fee
- title insurance/fee
- attorney fee
- lender fee
- lender points
- underwriter fee
- recording fee
- transfer stamps/fee
- property inspection/fee
- homeowner's insurance (must have this coverage before closing)
- local real estate taxes – prepayments and/or due
- primary mortgage insurance (PMI) – prepayment
- accrued mortgage interest between the closing date and 1st month's mortgage payment

This is a general outline that may give you some insight into the home buying process. Buying a home is not as hard as you might think. You just need to gather all requested information that will be asked of you to complete the process.

If you already own a home and have a mortgage with a high adjustable rate, you can consider refinancing it. You may be able to lock in a lower fixed interest rate and lower your monthly payments. Thus saving you thousands of dollars over time. (See Appendix for mortgage information resources).

Home Equity Options

If you have equity in your home, you can tap into your equity with one of two types of home equity loans; Home Equity Loan and Home Equity Line of Credit. These types of loans should only be done in dire situations; examples medical bills or needed home improvement/repair. Remember if you paid cash for your home, you automatically have equity to borrow against.

A Home Equity Loan is also known as a second mortgage. You get the entire amount you borrow up front. They typically have a fixed interest rate and a fixed monthly repayment schedule. You must start making payments on the loan as soon as you receive the funds.

A Home Equity Line of Credit (HELOC) is a type of loan where you are extended a line of credit based on the amount of equity you have in your home. You are only required to pay back the amount of the line (plus interest) you actually use. As long as you have not used any of the available credit line you are not required to make any payments.

Your interest rate with the HELOC is usually tied to the prime interest rate. If you have excellent credit, your interest rate could be as low as prime rate minus 1%; example: if the prime interest rate is 5%, your interest rate will be 4%. If you have bad credit, your rate can be as high as prime plus 2% (e.g. 7%) or more. Most HELOC`s are interest-only repayment plans for a set number of years (e.g. 10 years). Your payment does not go toward the principal, only the interest. You can apply additional payments toward the principal amount to speed up your repayment process. The annual percentage rate on a home equity loan or home equity line of credit in most cases is lower than the annual percentage rate on a credit card and may also be a tax write-off.

Property Tax Relief

Property tax rates for real estate are assessed differently in downtown major metropolitan areas versus suburbia or rural areas. Before purchasing a property, you should know what the taxes are and budget accordingly for this expense. Property taxes are used for several things like supporting local schools, park districts, and municipalities. The tax assessor's office determines the amount of property taxes to be paid by the owner.

Some properties that sit side by side pays different amounts of property taxes for many reasons. Unfortunately, also for various reasons (e.g. property reassessment, special community improvements, local tax rate increase), your property taxes can increase significantly without warning. If you feel your property taxes are too high, there should be a process within your local tax assessor's office that allows you to appeal your property tax assessment.

An incorrect property description or over-evaluation are only two reasons for appealing. These may not be the only reasons. Whatever your claim is that will bolster your chances to lower your property taxes, it is your responsibility to pursue this with the tax authority. You can save a significant amount of money on your taxes thereby adding more money to use for other purposes such as debt reduction, savings, etc.

If you choose the DIY property tax relief filing method, you will need comparable real estate information from similar properties in your area to help support your claim for reduction. Or you can seek out a professional property tax attorney that has the expertise, skill and knowledge to navigate through this process on your behalf. There may be a fee required so be sure to do your research and due diligence to understand all cost associated with their services.

INCOME PRODUCING PROPERTY

Income producing property that can bring in positive cash flow has been one of the oldest ways to gain financial freedom. It is one of the most common sources of passive income; i.e. letting your assets work for you. Income property allows you to use other people's money to pay off your debt and support your lifestyle. You can use the positive cash flow to get completely out of debt, pay the mortgage on that dream home you always wanted, take vacations, put your kids through college or whatever else you can dream of.

Remember the game Monopoly? According to history, Monopoly has actually been around for over 100 years, it's a redesign of an earlier game; "The Landlord's Game" first published by political activist Elizabeth Magie in 1903. The original intent of the game was to show that rents enriched property owners and impoverished tenants.

Despite Magie's original and renewed patents, several versions of the game were made and published in the years before the game was released by the Parker Brothers. The Parker Brother's version was re-named Monopoly in the 1930's.

If you landed on a property like Boardwalk, Park Place, or Pennsylvania Ave you had to pay luxury rent. That's why you try to buy as many properties as possible during the game. The player that ends up with the most money wins the game usually because he or she owns the most property. Sound familiar?

In the real world, vast fortunes have and continue to be created from real estate investing. New generations of billionaires are being created by inheriting these fortunes from their parents. Others are self-made by purchasing distressed property at a low cost and putting it back on the market for a huge profit.

A close friend (Mike Woods-Century 21 Real Estate Agent) informed me about his 5/F strategy for purchasing real estate from the investor point of view. His 5/F strategy is:

- Go **Find It**-under market value/profit available after completing the scope of work cost estimate.
- Go **Funky**-somewhat of an eye (nose) sore with great fix-up potential.
- Go **Fund It**-get prequalified using OPM-other's people's money or pay cash because cash is king.

- Go **Fix It**-RTW, right things wrong or easy low out of pocket fixes for maximum return on your investment dollar.
- Go **Farm It**-sale, rent or rent to own.

Unfortunately, during the housing meltdown starting in 2008, foreclosures were rising at a rapid rate causing millions of homeowners to walk away from their properties. They just could not afford the mortgage payments and upkeep. They had to enter the renter's market. The misfortune of some has provided others with tremendous opportunities in the real estate investors market.

The purchase of income producing property is still considered a good investment as long as the property can financially take care of itself, as well as pay you a profit. You could receive a passive stream of income from the monthly rentals on your property. The income should be enough to pay the property expenses (mortgage, insurance, maintenance, taxes, etc.) as well as provide you with additional cash flow.

Another potential advantage of owning rental property is Section 8, a government guaranteed housing voucher program that pays a majority of the rent for the tenant. The tenant is also responsible for a portion of the rent. The property must meet the standards set by the government to receive payment. Section 8 property owners must pass several inspections throughout the year to keep the property listed in the program.

While there are many benefits to income producing property, there are some disadvantages. One thing to remember is that you are liable for all of the expenses on the property even if it is not generating any income. Be sure to do a proper analysis of the earning potential of the property before purchasing it.

Income producing property ownership, along with reduced debt and good credit, can put you on the road to financial freedom. Income producing property comes with its challenges, but the reward for the risk could be well worth the undertaking. It is in your best interest to consult real estate investment professionals before investing in income producing property.

OTHER REAL ESTATE RELATED INVESTMENT OPTIONS

Beyond just owning a home or rental property, the real estate market has other ways one can earn a profit and build wealth. Care and due diligence should be done before investing in any venture. Be sure to consult with an experienced financial expert. Following is a brief description of some of those options.

Rehab/Resell (aka Flipping)

Basically, you acquire "fixer-upper" houses or any property that is generally unwanted by the average homebuyer. You repair the property and put it back on the market for profitable resale. Of course the techniques used to find and acquire such properties vary widely; searching websites for foreclosure properties, using realtors, attending real estate auctions, negotiating short sales or using referral partners. Rehabbing properties is not a passive strategy, it is an active business, so be prepared.

Wholesaling

Wholesaling is a sub-category of flipping in which you are the middleman. It is an active business in which:

1. A motivated seller is located. They could be motivated due to pending foreclosure, inherited property, relocating or other reasons.
2. You construct a solution that involves the negotiated sale of that property to you at a discount or some other favorable financial terms. The seller should receive some value from the deal making it a win-win situation.
3. You put the property under contract (or purchase it outright), with the intention of a quick resale to another investor at wholesale prices. You negotiate your fee/ payment from the deal with your investor. You should

ensure your investor has the funds to acquire the
property from you. Ask them to provide a current
dated proof of funds from their financial institution on
their letterhead or a valid cashier's check.

Tax Lien Investing

Once property taxes are delinquent for a given period of
time, the county government offers tax lien certificates on
their delinquent properties. As investors, you can acquire
tax lien certificates that pay fixed rates of returns from 8%
to 36% interest per year depending on which county you're
investing in. You don't need to go to auctions to acquire tax
lien certificates. You can buy tax lien certificates directly from
the county or use a reputable service.

When you acquire the tax lien certificate, you are paying
the delinquent property tax bill instead of the property owner.
You become the first position lien holder of record. When the
delinquent property taxes are paid by the property owner,
you receive all of your original investment back, plus interest
based on a guaranteed interest rate (e.g. 8% to 36%).

Each state has a redemption period or grace period
in which the delinquent property taxes must be paid.
Redemption periods range from 6 months to 3 years
depending on which county you're investing in. If the
delinquent property taxes are not paid within the redemption
period, then the property will be taken through a judicial
process (property tax foreclosure). Once this process is
complete, you will own the property outright and receive a
free and clear deed to the property.

Lastly, keep in mind that profitable real estate investing
does not begin until your money, rather than your time and
activity, begin to make more money (i.e. profit) for you.

REFINANCING OPTIONS TO KEEP YOUR HOME

Depending on your age and financial situation I want to
mention three Federal Government programs that might be
of assistance to you. If you are looking for mortgage relief
the Home Affordable Refinance Program-H.A.R.P., the Home

Affordable Modification Program and the Reverse Mortgage Program might be able to assist you.

All three programs offer different services and have different requirements and qualifications. If you meet the standards of eligibility, you can participate in the program that best serves your need. Only you can be the judge of that! Let's begin with H.A.R.P.

Home Affordable Refinance Program-H.A.R.P

H.A.R.P is a federal program which allows homeowners, who are eligible, and who owe more on their mortgage than the house is worth (high loan to value ratio) to refinance into a more affordable (lower) or stable (fixed) rate currently available. Thereby, reducing their current monthly mortgage payment. The H.A.R.P application deadline has been extended until December 31th, 2016.

In 2009, the H.A.R.P program accepted borrowers whose loan to value ratio was higher than 80 percent. Then the program grew, to include borrowers with 125 percent loan to value. In 2011, the new H.A.R.P 2.0 had no limits on the amount of negative equity for mortgages up to thirty years and allowed you to change lenders to refinance. The Federal Government will not hold the new lender responsible for any fraudulent action that might have transpired in connection with the original loan.

The second way you can benefit from the H.A.R.P is from converting your Adjustable Rate Mortgage (ARM) into a fixed rate loan. You can also choose to refinance at a shorter term than your original term, i.e. from a 30-year ARM to a 25, 20, 15, 10-year fixed rate loan. This could save you thousands of dollars in interest and payments over the length of the new H.A.R.P.

Check with your current lending institution which services your mortgage loan and see what options are available to you. There are a vast number of choices out there depending on your eligibility.

Home Affordable Modification Program-H.A.M.P

This is a program for homeowners who are in great financial danger of foreclosure. They are current on mortgage payments but are unable to refinance due to the steady decline in home prices.

This program can provide relief for eligible participants who suffered from unaffordable increases in expenses and/ or reduction in their income. To qualify for the H.A.M.P program, you must show financial hardship and purchased your home before January 1st of 2009. You cannot have any convictions within the last 10 years like theft, fraud or forgery just to name a few. See your mortgage company for specific details.

Reverse Mortgage

According to the website (www.hud.gov), the Home Equity Conversion Mortgage (H.E.C.M) is the Federal Housing Authority's (FHA) reverse mortgage program. A reverse mortgage is a special type of home loan that allows qualified seniors age 62 and older to convert the equity in their home into cash. The equity that they have built up over years of making mortgage payments can now be paid to them.

Unlike a traditional home equity loan or second mortgage, H.E.C.M borrowers do not have to repay the H.E.C.M loan until the borrowers no longer use the home as their primary residence (e.g. death or move to a nursing home) or fail to meet the obligations of the loan. The loan is charged interest on the amount received. The interest is compounded over the life of the loan and added to the principal amount borrowed. You can also use the proceeds from H.E.C.M to purchase another primary residence.

To be eligible for an H.E.C.M loan, the FHA requires that you be a homeowner 62 years of age or older and own your home outright, or have a low mortgage balance that can be paid off at closing with proceeds from the loan. You must live in the home. You must also have the financial resources to pay ongoing property expenses including taxes and insurance.

You are also required to receive consumer information free or at a low cost from an H.E.C.M counselor prior to obtaining the loan. You can find a counselor via the website (www.hud.gov).

A reverse mortgage loan provides the homeowner with a lump sum payment, fixed monthly payments or as a line of credit per the contract agreement. You will keep the title and always own your home for the full duration of the loan.

You can pay off some debts, make home improvements or help your children or grandchildren. Or maybe you want to take a flight to London, stay in a five-star hotel and go shopping. You can catch the Orient Express passenger rail car from London to Paris, then on to Monaco on the French Rivera and stay in the beautiful city of Monte Carlo overlooking the Mediterranean Sea. The sky (loan amount) is the limit!

The H.E.C.M is a safe plan that can give older Americans greater financial security. Many seniors use it to supplement Social Security, meet unexpected medical expenses, and make home improvements, travel, etc.

You should also be aware that there are drawbacks to reverse mortgages. In addition to high fees and high mortgage interest rates for reverse mortgages, the debt will become the responsibility of the living heirs. They will need to pay back the original loan plus accrued interest. If they don't have the funds, they will need to sell the home and use the proceeds to satisfy the balance due.

In addition to the website (www.hud.gov), you can get additional free information about reverse mortgages by contacting the National Council on Aging (NCOA) or downloading their free booklet, "Use Your Home to Stay at Home," a guide for older homeowners who need help now. You can search NCOA website for reverse mortgage information. Or contact the National Reverse Mortgage Lenders Association.

Do your research. It is smart to know more about reverse mortgages and decide if one is right for you! If you decide a reverse mortgage is right for you, you will have some cash to do as you please and enjoy your senior years without the burden of a mortgage.

Please be aware that the above three government sponsored programs were available at the time this book was published. The government can eliminate any or all of these programs or create new ones at any time. Be sure to check which government or community programs are available to help protect your home at the time you need assistance. (See Appendix for program contact information).

FORECLOSURE AND SHORT SALES

Short Sale

When a homeowner is unable to make mortgage payments, one option is to sell, but sometimes a homeowner owes more than the house is worth. This creates a problem for both the homeowner and the lender. Both parties can resolve such issues through a short sale, which takes place during the pre-foreclosure phase.

A short sale allows you as a homeowner to sell your home for less than you owe once you become financially unable to repay all the outstanding liens on the home.

All lien holders (i.e. banks) must agree to release the liens on the property and accept less than the total amount of debt owed by the borrower.

Please note that Short Sale agreements do not necessarily release the borrower from their financial obligations to repay any portion of the unpaid balance remaining. You the borrower and the lender both must agree in writing (contract form) or as state laws dictate, how the remaining portion will be paid.

I recommend that you consult a real estate attorney with foreclosure expertise. Here is a sample listing of things an attorney will or should go over with you during the beginning stages a short sale process. The list includes, but is not limited to the following:

- authorization – this document allows the release of information to a designated person i.e.; your attorney or designee appointed by your attorney such as a paralegal.

- hardship letter - is submitted to the lender on your behalf, giving you a chance to explain why you are unable to pay your mortgage (e.g. loss of one or both incomes, divorce or separation, etc.)
- last two check stubs
- last two years of income tax returns
- last two bank statements
- other documents as requested

You must take into consideration that short sales can be cumbersome and time-consuming at best. It can take anywhere from two months to two years, even longer depending on all parties coming to an agreement. A short sale is often used as an alternative to foreclosure because it mitigates additional fees and costs to both the creditor and borrower.

Foreclosure

Foreclosure is a legal process where the mortgage holder can repossess or sell the property for repayment of the debt owed on that property. Mortgage holders can foreclose anytime after the borrower starts missing payments on the mortgage per the terms of the agreement, or per the laws of the state where the property is located. All options for saving your home should be explored before getting to the Foreclosure process, if possible.

As reported in the media and the internet, in 2008, the housing market collapsed leading to the largest foreclosure rate in the history of the United States. The collapse was due to the Subprime Mortgage crisis caused by the banking industry. I will not attempt to explain the details of this crisis in this book. One could write an entire book on this subject alone. You can easily search the internet for "Housing Crisis" and get a plethora of details.

The goal here is to inform you that in the event you are facing a foreclosure and/or short sale (see below) situation you do have legal rights. It is critical that you know and understand these rights. Both homeowners and renters have rights.

In some foreclosure cases, homeowners try to work out an arrangement with the lender hoping to get back on track with late payments. If the homeowner can't catch up as well as keep up with current payments, and cannot refinance the original loan, the lender can start foreclosure proceedings. After some time, the homeowner is issued a move out notice or is forcefully evicted from their home.

Unfortunately, too many choose to try and work with the bank in a desperate effort to save the home. What happens too often is that homeowners ignore the legal process in the courts, give up their rights to defend the foreclosure and are turned down by the bank at the last minute.

Homeowners, even if they miss payments on a loan, have the right to defend their home and demand that the bank follow strict procedures and laws before it can take a home through foreclosure. These rights must be presented in court before the sheriff sale of the property is scheduled and ownership of the property is transferred back to the bank or a new owner.

If homeowners do not defend their rights, the foreclosure process can take just a few months. But simply by standing up for their rights in a foreclosure, homeowners may be able to drag out the process by many additional months or even years. And in some cases they will be able to leave the home on their own terms if it comes to that.

While all homeowners have some rights related to foreclosure, how these rights work may differ slightly in judicial and non-judicial foreclosure states. Banks must also follow all of the applicable laws that govern mortgage lending, and violations of these laws may be violations of homeowners' rights. Generally, in some states, lenders must initiate a lawsuit in court to foreclose. In non-judicial states, a lender may foreclose without a lawsuit in court but must abide by the notice requirements in that state.

Foreclosure Assistance

In response to the housing crisis and the millions of homeowners facing foreclosure, the Making Home Affordable Program was initiated by the Obama administration. The Making Home Affordable Program (MHA) is a critical part of the Obama Administration's broad strategy to help homeowners avoid foreclosure and stabilize the country's housing market. The overall goal is to improve the nation's economy by keeping more money in your pocket to spend on products, goods, and services.

The Department of the Treasury and the U.S. Department of Housing and Urban Development encouraged leaders in the lending industry, investors, and non-profits to form an alliance. HOPE (Home Owners Preserving Equity) "NOW" is an alliance between counselors, mortgage companies, investors, and other mortgage market participants.

This alliance will maximize outreach efforts to homeowners in distress to help them stay in their homes and will create a unified, coordinated plan to reach out and help as many homeowners as possible. The members of this alliance recognize that by working together, they will be more effective than by working independently.

If you know someone or if you are currently behind on your mortgage or facing foreclosure you can contact HOPE NOW to get free advice from a housing expert. HUD-approved housing counselors work with you and your mortgage company on your behalf, and their expertise is available for free. Visit HOPE NOW website (www.hopenow.com) for a full list of Alliance members and to contact an expert about your individual situation.

Be aware that predatory lending has been said to be an important factor in the countless number of rising foreclosures across America today. There has been a surge in fraud related to foreclosure assistance for consumers. Always check the validity of the company with your State's Attorney General's office before doing business with them. Avoid companies which:

- Claim they are mortgage consultants;
- Ask you to pay an advance fee before they are able to perform any service for you;
- Claim they can stop the foreclosure proceeding if you are in default and rescue your property;
- Take over your house at a discount;

- Tell you to pay the company instead of your lender;
- Tell you to transfer your deed to the company; or
- Anyone who claims they will give you a good deal

If you need help, put your pride to the side and make the call. Save your home! But be sure to consult an attorney and/or foreclosure/short sale experts in your area first. Also, be sure to confirm that these government programs are still available at the time you need them. (See Appendix for foreclosure information resources).

And lastly, you should also be aware of the impact that foreclosure and short sales will have on your credit report and score.

REMEMBER, "THE BEST IMPROVEMENT STARTS WITH SELF IMPROVEMENT."

POEM - HALFWAY POINT

The halfway point, keep reading more

You might read something that will open a door

As you read on, keep an open mind

Some of your issues might be similar to mine

This book is about how I changed my life

I share with you how I paid a heavy price

Don't be ashamed if you failed to plan

This book is offering a helping hand

In your spare time, you might want to

Make a list of things you need to work through

If you need a change, you will know

If you make no effort in the end, it will show!

-MICHAEL "BART" MATHEWS

CHAPTER 6
BUILDING WEALTH: ENTREPRENEURSHIP

"Whatever the mind can conceive and believe,
it can achieve."

– NAPOLEON HILL

CAPITALISM

ACCORDING TO THE Miriam Webster dictionary, Capitalism is defined as "an economic system characterized by private or corporate ownership of capital goods, by investments that are determined by private decision, and by prices, production and the distribution of goods that are determined mainly by competition in the free market." In other words, capitalism gives John or Jane Doe the opportunity to pull him or herself up by their bootstraps by creating a product or service for sale with the intent to profit. Without capitalism by way of private citizens starting a business and selling goods and services for profit, where would we be today?

People from all over the world continue to flock to America because of two words, CAPITALISM and FREEDOM. The Statue of Liberty on Liberty Island is a worldwide symbol of hope and prosperity. Foreigners, seek out the shores of the United States in hopes of living the same American dream that every countryman and naturalized citizen have the right to live. Capitalism has spread globally in developed and underdeveloped countries.

There is a difference between a capitalist and an entrepreneur. A venture capitalist provides the capital (investment money) to entrepreneurs to start businesses. Capitalism gets a bad wrap because some wealthy individuals and corporations take advantage of other people and tax loopholes to continue to grow wealthy and not pay their fair share to support society at large. Not all capitalist are like that. There are capitalists with a "conscience". They do contribute to society in an effort to improve the economic conditions of others. They start charitable foundations and or donate large sums of money to other charitable organizations. Don't let the actions of some stop you from becoming an entrepreneur or a venture capitalist with a "conscience"!

ENTREPRENEURSHIP

Entrepreneurship is the process of starting a business or organization. The entrepreneur develops a business model, acquires human and other resources, and is entirely responsible for its success or failure.

Entrepreneurs are self-starters who take advantage of capitalism. Some millionaires' even billionaires are self-made by becoming entrepreneurs. They first came up with a vision and then an idea of what to do to make the vision a reality. The idea was then turned into a concept for success.

Next, they created a written plan of action that would guide them closer toward accomplishing their goals. Add marketing, a brick, and mortar and/or online e-commerce store, now the business or dream is up and running. Lastly, and most importantly, their product or service is now available in the marketplace for sale with the intent on making a profit. Why? Because of capitalism and the free enterprise system.

The well-planned entrepreneur is fortunate to have a stash of cash and started his or her business with money they saved. Some start-ups used OPM, other people's money by borrowing from family, friends or credit cards, or partnering with other like-minded outside of the box thinkers allowing them to take their idea, goal or dream to the next level.

If you can learn the financial basics for starting a business including how much it will cost and what it takes to run one, your household can be your corporation. By investing and creating products and/or services in your kitchen, basement or garage that result in sales for profit, you are well on your way to starting your family business.

For me, my wife was and still is the most significant investment that I have ever made as an adult. I say this because we are a team (entrepreneurs) and we share the same vision (partners) in the present as well as for our future. We walk side by side in all that we do with the full understanding of what we are trying to achieve.

The haters will hate on you and your efforts to become successful from wealth building because your vision is not understandable to them. Some will stab you in the back with the same amount of effort it takes to smile in your face. They will say things like, "Who do you think you are?", "You are no better than me!", "You are not going to amount to anything," "You are only wasting your time", or my favorite "Man, you are crazy, you can't do that!" Some will actually stop associating with you but keep watching from the sidelines hoping you will fail so they can say "I know you couldn't do it" or "I told you so"!

That is known as the "crabs in the barrel syndrome." When one crab finally makes it to the edge of the barrel with an escape from the rat race in sight. Another crab will grab its claw and pull it back down with all the rest of the crabs who are unwilling to try to escape from the rat race. Crabs are similar to some people who never get off the porch to run with the big dogs in life.

Instead of getting in the game of life and giving life a real shot at success, they stand idle on the sidelines and watch life pass them by. They try to bring you down with them. To share your ideas, goals and dreams with them can be an emotional kiss of death. Hold on to your dreams close to your heart until you are ready for the world to know. Some will, some won`t, some do, some don`t, but everyone can if you believe! *"It's crowded at the bottom, so why not climb to the top." - Les Brown.*

Owning your own business is no longer just an American dream, it is a global dream that can be realized. Other countries worldwide have their share of successful entrepreneurs as you can see from Forbes list of billionaires. So you have a world of opportunity right at your fingertips. You can turn on your iPad, tablet, laptop or desktop even your smartphone and sell your goods or services anywhere in the world using the internet.

The same goes for you corporate climbers when climbing the ladder of success reaching for the glass ceiling. Do you find that the glass ceiling is hard as cement? Your progress is stopped and you can no longer advance within the company you spent 10, 20 even 30 years working for. If you can't reach that ceiling, there are plenty more ladders for you to climb if you want it bad enough. You must be willing to step out on faith and be prepared for the opportunity!

How do you look at the glass of life, as being half full of opportunity and you are rising to the top? Or half empty, filled with road blocks and you are sinking down to the bottom? How many ideas have come to mind that you did not do anything about? Or have you witnessed one of your ideas put into reality by someone who decided to take action.

No matter what anybody says, every business startup stepped out on faith because someone had an idea and the tenacity to get out of their comfort zone and venture out into the vast sea of opportunity. Along the road to success, you will lose plenty of friends, just because they are not driven toward being successful beyond working a nine to five job. But you will gain access to a new circle of friends that will appreciate your drive, ambition, and success.

Remember, "No Risk, No Reward."

PHILANTHROPY

"A sure way for one to lift himself up is by
helping to lift up someone else."
-BOOKER T WASHINGTON

Your conscience is an inner feeling, intuition, voice, or judgment of morality that is viewed or is used as a guide to the rightness or wrongness of one's behavior.

This is what the American dream is all about. One has the opportunity to become anything that he or she wants, in spite of their birthplace, current circumstances, race, color or creed, from his or her own efforts. But sometimes you might need a little help.

Being wealthy whether through entrepreneurship or not is not a bad thing. However, there is a saying that "when much is given much is expected." There is an expectation that you are obligated to give back and reach back to those that are less fortunate once you become wealthy. I believe that all of us have a duty to give back either time or money to help society progress. Especially if you are wealthy. Social consciousness has come into play for some individuals, couples, and corporations who have amassed a vast amount of wealth.

Andrew Carnegie (millionaire-philanthropist) wrote an article over 125 years ago in 1889 stating "The Gospel of Wealth" which was his way of asking rich people to use their wealth to improve society. Carnegie made hundreds of millions of dollars in the steel industry before giving away upwards of 90% of his fortune to charities, foundations and universities. Andrew Carnegie passed his humanitarian philosophy onto successful men like Henry Ford, Napoleon Hill, and modern day wealth holders Bill/Melinda Gates, and Warren Buffett. Together, they started "The Giving Pledge." It is a campaign to encourage the wealthiest (billionaires) around the world to make a commitment to give most of their wealth to philanthropic (charitable) causes. On June 2nd, 2015 a CNBC article discussed the list of billionaires or former billionaire's, individuals and couples who signed the Giving Pledge. From the initial list of 40 families, the current list of willing, voluntary participants was now at 137. The Giving Pledge is a moral commitment to give and not a legal binding contract. Their efforts help make this world a better place for deserving men, women and children so they can live a better life.

Using the rewards of capitalism, you can start your own foundation and share your philanthropic vision of service in your own special way. Or, you can support a well-established organization that is already providing the type of community outreach opportunities that are near and dear to your heart.

My point is this, the more wealth that you accumulate you are afforded a better opportunity to reach back and help others. The higher up the economic ladder you climb, the more people you can help with the service-driven cause of your choice! But we don't need to be billionaires to start, not even millionaires. All you need is a philanthropic heart and consciousness! Make philanthropy a part of your wealth legacy!

REMEMBER,"THE BEST IMPROVEMENT STARTS WITH SELF IMPROVEMENT."

POEM - ENTREPRENEURSHIP

From Andrew Carnegie to Napoleon Hill

Entrepreneurs have flourished, from determination and

sheer will

From Jobs to Zuckerburg, Winfrey, and Gates

Entrepreneurs are still growing at alarming rates

You have an idea, now start your business

Like millions before you, who also bare witness

Use market research, identify and learn more

When will your dream open up its door

Use mastermind groups, evaluate what they say

Is your plan solid, do you forge on the same way

Now you possess your burning desire

You will continue to soar higher and higher

Always persist, I'm sure you've been told

The keys to success, in your heart you do hold

Entrepreneurs often think outside of the box

Keep on learning, become smart like a fox

With a positive mental attitude and your thick skin

If you never quit, in the end you will win

-MICHAEL "BART" MATHEWS

CHAPTER 7
PLANNING FOR YOUR FUTURE

*"You were born to win but to be a winner,
you must plan to win, prepare to win, and
expect to win."*

-ZIG ZIGLAR

FINANCIAL PLANNING

OR YEARS, MY wife and I thought we were doing the right thing because we made plans for our future. Together we saved and invested while approaching our retirement years. One day we decided to seek a professional review from a financial planner to ensure that our plans were solid. We needed a second opinion to validate if we were on the right track to obtaining Financial Freedom for Life.

Once our financial planner reviewed our financial information, we quickly realized two important factors. The first revelation was we found out we were actually on the right track with our personal savings. The second revelation was that we were in too much debt and needed to eliminate it

135

before we retired. So she told us exactly what we had to do, to get to the next level.

Financially Speaking, we realized there was more work to be done for us to get to where we wanted to be, from a financial standpoint. If you are married, you and your spouse should be on one accord and make all major financial decisions together. You can both agree to disagree, but the bottom line is everyone should have at least a general financial snapshot of where you both stand. If you are single, the same is true for you.

In order to reach our retirement goals, our planner made several suggestions that helped our financial goals become more of a reality and a meaningful specific. We shared an excellent working relationship with our financial planner. I have a question for you. Do you think you should have a financial plan? You can put the blame on others for your financial situation, but isn't it about time to accept personal responsibility for your future by making a plan?

Financial Planning is the process to establish an action plan for building wealth, growing wealth and protecting your wealth. Retirement is one of the most motivating reasons for people to begin financial planning, but not the only reason. Retirement is based on <u>money,</u> not age. Only Social Security is based on age or disability. If you had the wealth to retire today, would you keep on going to work regardless of your age?

Some people would say "Yes" just because they enjoy their line of work. But I bet that most people would jump at the chance to walk away from the hassles and stress of the workplace environment. Wouldn't you prefer to start living the life of leisure, financial freedom, and service that is everyone's dream?

Maybe you might want to take a cruise for several months, or maybe you might want to pay off your home and become debt free and never worry about living expenses. What about paying off that student loan or purchasing that dream car? Or would you start a charitable foundation and help others who are in a transitional period in their life? We all want different things in life, but without a financial plan to go along with your goals and dreams; your actual journey to financial freedom and happiness could be a difficult challenge. Don't leave your financial success to chance, be proactive.

Of course, you already do some type of financial planning. Paying your bills and just making ends meet is a form of financial planning. But this form leaves out the most important part, and that part is you.

Once you decide to make a financial plan, you basically need to reduce/eliminate debt and build a portfolio that contains the right mix of saving, and investment options that can help you reach your goals. You can research and figure it out on your own. This will require proper financial knowledge, time, and commitment or you can go to a certified or licensed financial planner.

What Should I Expect From A Financial Planner?

The financial planner of your choice will advise you based upon the information you give them. So it is imperative that you be totally honest with your information no matter how bad your situation might seem to you. Remember the goal of a financial planner is to help you develop a written plan of action that will help you achieve your goals and dreams. Financial planning, whether done by yourself or a professional planner should be a lifelong process.

Financial planners will review your sources of income, your assets, each liabilities/debt along with the interest rates you are paying, and net worth. They will evaluate all your insurance plans, estate plan, tax returns, pretax investments, your after-tax investments, and emergency savings needs. Also, they will look into bonds, stocks and other investment vehicles that can help you reach your goals and build a stronger financial future.

Many people, more than you realize, spend more money than they earn and are buried in debt. Learning to pay down your debt as well as building a sizable nest egg by investing can help you to maintain the standard of living you desire. The financial planner can help develop your debt and expense reduction plan as well.

Financial planning should be a must for everyone. Do you realize how many people you know that have never done any short, medium or long-term financial planning? What about you, have you taken on this undertaking of financial planning? I know you have heard the phrase, "You must pull yourself up by your bootstraps." Well, your financial bootstraps may also need some tightening up. I cannot stress enough that you should take an in-depth look at your overall financial picture and see where you stand. My main point is that if you fail to learn, you might fail to earn at your full potential.

A good planner, upon review of the financial information you provide, will make suggestions or changes for you to consider. Remember the planner works for you and the final decision will be yours to make. A financial planner is like a coach of a basketball team. The coach will draw up a play, and you will have the responsibility of executing it. A good financial planner can draw up your financial play and be your coach at the same time. But in the end, it's totally up to you to execute the plan once it is received by taking immediate action.

What Type Of Financial Planning Services Will I Receive?

Depending on the arrangement you have with the planner, you could receive any or all of the following types of services:

- tax planning and preparation
- estate planning
- debt and expense reduction plan
- investment options and recommendations
- retirement planning
- cash planning
- insurance planning/long term care
- health planning
- wealth building options

How Will I Be Charged For the Financial Planner's Services?

You should obtain a written statement or contract that indicates all fees for the services you will be provided along with the method of payment. You don't want to complete any part of your financial planning services without knowing what it will cost upfront. Ask for a full list of all fees and services for your review. You might want to do a cost comparison analysis of about three or four other financial planners for the exact same service you are seeking. This should give you a price range to choose from.

You also want to know how many return visits you will be entitled to, along with the length of the term of your partnership. A one-to-two-year relationship is a good start. That should give your planner the time needed to give you a plan of action for your financial roadmap going forward. Your newfound financial roadmap for success will be monitored and adjusted based on the many different life changes you will encounter in between visits.

What Can Take Place At The First Meeting?

Your first meeting is usually the icebreaker, to get to know one another. You will try to establish a trusting relationship and decide if you would like to continue working together. You and the planner should agree upon a time and place to meet. The planner might suggest meeting at your home or an in office visit might be required. I recommend the office visit.

This will help you see a brick and mortar office building as a base of business operation. Look around at everything, from college degrees to certificates hanging on the walls, the level of foot traffic coming in and out as well as the number of people working in this business setting. Some planners also work from a home base; just make sure they are legitimate and come with references.

Topics that should be discussed in this first session are your short, medium, and long-term goals. Discuss what is most important to you. You should consider "Am I comfortable working with this person?" "Is this person knowledgeable enough to address my goals?" "Are the fees reasonable?" Remember you have the final say. Take your time, ask as many questions as you deem necessary. No question is a dumb a question. The only dumb question is the one you never ask. You have nothing to lose and everything to gain in terms of additional knowledge. Be a good listener, and take notes for later review and research.

You will probably leave that first meeting with much more knowledge than when you first came in, and at this point you may not have spent one cent. A good planner will scratch the surface to assure you that he/she will cover all the areas of planning if you decide to retain their services. After the first meeting, you and your significant other will need to determine next steps. Thoroughly review the information you received from the meeting and based on your current situation and your goals, make a decision on how you wish to proceed.

How to Find and Select a Financial Planner

There are several hundred if not thousands of financial planners. Many work for Fortune 500 companies and possess the professional expertise to offer a broad range of services. However, one of the best ways to find a financial planner is by word of mouth from people you trust and respect. If that person is satisfied with the services received, they will probably be happy to give you a personal referral.

Many financial planners will grant you a free initial consultation. However, before anything is discussed, you need to verify that they are licensed and registered with the Securities and Exchange Commission (SEC). Ask to see all documented licenses and registrations. They should explicitly state that this person or company is registered with the SEC. The planner's licenses should show that they have passed the required local, state, and/or federal licensing exams or certifications.

The SEC has a set of rules and regulations in place for your protection in case of misrepresentation on behalf of the financial planner. If no registration is produced, then thank them and end your conversation. This initial free consultation will enable you to do your research and check the credentials of the company or person with whom you might entrust your personal financial information. There are several types of planners, but I will focus on the Certified Financial Planner.

The Certified Financial Planner is a trained personal finance specialist who has been certified by the Financial Board of Standards. The requirements for certification consist of the planner having three years of client experience, complete a series of CFP Board-registered courses, and passing a two-day, 10-hour exam. You might want to know the planner's college and graduate degrees and what were their areas of study. You might ask about their continuing education requirements. You might also request references from other clients who were serviced.

You should ask who will be working directly with you during your financial planning sessions. Has the financial planner taken the fiduciary oath? The fiduciary oath means that the advisor of your choice will put forth his or her best efforts to act in good faith and have your best interest as their number one concern.

I mentioned earlier about getting referrals for financial planners from friends and family members. Word of mouth for a job well done is as good as it gets. So start asking around first. You can go to your local chamber of commerce or local library for sources of reference. You can also contact any number of professional organizations that will assist you such as:

- The National Association of Personal Financial Planning.
- The Financial Planning Association.
- The Personal Financial Planning Division.
- The Society of Financial Service Professionals.

(See Appendix for financial professionals information resources).

What do you have to lose by contacting the financial planner of your choice? Remember, knowledge is power. Information and knowledge will enable you to be more informed and select the best financial planner possible.

RETIREMENT PLANNING

There has been an ongoing and growing fear among millions of American workers that their company pension plans might not be around when they retire. With fund managers borrowing (or misappropriation/embezzlement of funds) money from pension plans and many baby boomers retiring and drawing their pensions, there was a high potential for a shortfall in the overall remaining pension funds to service all pensioners. Well, guess what happened in 2008.

As a result of the 2008 economic crisis, many businesses that offered pension plans could no longer afford them and therefore, dissolved, or changed the plan altogether. The billions invested in high-risk securities became worthless, the auto industry crisis, corporate bankruptcies (e.g. Goldman Sachs) the sub-prime mortgage market crisis, and the subsequent government bailouts all contributed to the stock market drop from 13,000 to 6,600, in March 2009.

Unfortunately, for the millions of Americans that actually planned for retirement using pension plans, IRAs, and 401k savings as their primary income during retirement lost their entire retirement portfolios or a large chunk of it. After working, 20, 25 or 30 plus years for the same company, many loyal and hardworking employees were being told that all their years of pension contributions were suddenly gone.

Also, with the massive wave of "Baby Boomers" (born 1945 to 1964) becoming eligible for retirement, there is growing concern about Social Security income not being available during retirement years. According to the Social Security Administration website (www.ssa.gov), "the combined assets of the Old-Age, Survivors Insurance and Disability Insurance (OASDI) Trust Funds are projected to be depleted in 2033, unchanged from 2012, with 77 percent of benefits still payable at that time."

"The Disability Income fund is predicted to deplete in 2016, also unchanged from 2012, with 80 percent of benefits still payable." So these fears, true or false, seem definitely justifiable. I don't know if this will actually occur, but what I do know is that if you have not already started to plan for your retirement, you are making a big mistake. You are committing financial suicide for failing to plan!

One day I had a conversation with a senior citizen while sitting at the end of the line on a Chicago Transit Authority bus in Chicago before I retired. He told me he was 68 years old, collecting Social Security and still could not afford to retire or stop working. He went on to say that over the 40 plus years of his working life, he never saved much and he had no other income stream to depend on.

Sure he saved a small amount of cash but he kept on spending what he made until his financial cushion went dry. He depleted his stash from underneath his mattress and had no investments. He did own a home with 10 years remaining before it would be paid off (he would be 78 years old). He has children, but they wanted nothing to do with him. He did not mention having a monthly pension check coming in to help supplement his income so I think that is why he was still working.

He is living from two sources of income: earned income from a part-time job, and fixed income from a social security check. However, he understands that when the time comes where he can no longer work and if social security does run out, he will be between a rock and a hard place. But until then, at least he has a roof over his head.

After hearing this story from a complete stranger, it compelled me to share his experience with you as well as step up my own wealth building and retirement planning action plan.

How many senior citizens do you know or see that appear to be having a difficult time with meeting basic living expenses while living on a fixed income? What makes you think things will change for you in your retirement years without a 40 hour a week paycheck coming in and no pension in place and no social security check? Your job is to avoid becoming like them.

Unfortunately, still today many senior citizens have not done any retirement planning at all. They are struggling to make ends meet because they lacked the necessary financial means to maintain a comfortable and dignified lifestyle. Or maybe they did earn decent income during their working careers but spent or lost all they made because of the lack of financial literacy or circumstances beyond their control. This should be a wake-up call for you (just as it was for me) to begin planning and setting your goals for retirement whether you are a senior or not.

Depending on your age, you may, or may not have had serious thoughts about when you will be able to retire? Where you will live when you retire? At what age you will be able to retire? How much money you will have and need to live on throughout your retirement years? I remember when I was in my twenties; I did not give retirement a first, second, or third thought. If I knew then what I know now, I would have started planning, saving and investing right then.

People are living longer and have fewer resources to live on as they get older. I am speaking to all Baby Boomers born from 1945 to 1964, if you are not currently retired, you might be retiring in a few short years. You have less time to take advantage of the power of wealth-building using multiple streams of income that would allow you to grow a sizeable retirement nest egg. But, it's better late than never.

Whether you want to retire in a grand jet-set, travel-filled come and go as you please world-wind lifestyle, or just be financially able to meet your monthly living expenses, you must still make a plan. With little socially economic choices, by failing to plan, unconsciously you plan to fail!

You might want to live in your current home during your retirement years. If you still owe a mortgage on your home when you stop working, will you be able to pay it along with the property taxes and all other living expenses? If you are renting, how long will you be able to keep on paying the landlord if or when your money runs out?

You might already be in a situation that requires you to assist one or both of your parents financially because they did not plan for retirement or for some other reasons no fault of their own doing. The possibility of an elder suffering from an illness and having no financial reserve or insurance in their time of need is a serious issue. Sure your parents might receive Social Security and/or disability income, and some might receive a pension, but it may not be sufficient for them to live on. Therefore, they may have to move in with you one day.

Are they self-sufficient or do they need special services and assistive devices to be mobile and ambulatory? Do they need assisted-care (long-term care insurance) living 24 hours a day? Is this a responsibility you want to pass on to your children?

You can gain first-hand information from your parents or grandparents experiences. Some may have done what it takes to retire and maintain a healthy financial stream of income throughout retirement. My dad worked for 40 years and retired with a full pension, social security benefits and our home was paid in full. However, he passed away at age 72 having only enjoyed seven years of retirement. From that experience, I set my retirement goal to be age 55 so I could enjoy more of my retirement years.

Others senior citizens might be struggling to make ends meet because of the lack of wealth-building and financial planning. You might want to talk to them about what went wrong. They might be a source of valuable information for you. My point is that you can see what happens if one lives long enough and does not plan for retirement.

Retirement planning should include, but not limited to: how you legally pay the smallest amount of taxes possible, a long-term fixed source of income, and wealth growth and preservation. The goal is to allow you to outlive your money. Also, depending upon your parents' situation, you may need to factor supporting them into your retirement planning process.

The goal is for you not to repeat the same mistakes that your grandparents or your parents might have made when it comes to retirement planning. While you are in your twenties, thirties or even forties, it is a good time to start your retirement planning. The earlier (younger) you start, the longer you have to enjoy the real magic of wealth creation and compound interest reinvested along with regular contributions that should grow your nest egg.

Don't allow your retirement years to become a wandering generality. Take steps now to ensure that your entire financial life is a meaningful specific. Start planning your retirement years today. You cannot afford to leave your retirement to chance or the government alone and hope all will turn out okay. If you do not plan for retirement today, you are taking a chance on your lifestyle of tomorrow.

In 2014, during the State of the Union address President Obama announced that he authorized the U.S. Treasury to create a new starter savings account called "myRA"(i.e. My Retirement Account). The objective was to help people get started saving again or for the first time. This starter savings account would stay with you if you changed jobs and would be backed by the U.S. Treasury. The target audience is millions of low and middle-income Americans who don't have access to employer-sponsored retirement plans or who are looking to supplement their current plan.

According to the U.S. Treasury (www.treasury.gov), married households earning up to $191,000 and individuals earning up to $129,000 can contribute up to $15,000 after-tax dollars for a maximum of 30 years, whichever comes first. The principal would be protected and can't go down in value. Interest could be based on the same variable interest rate as investments in the government securities fund for federal employees.

Contributions would be made via payroll tax deductions or directly from your checking and savings accounts. It can start with as little as $25 dollars and contribute as little as $5 per pay period.

Withdrawals can be made tax-free at any time without penalty under certain circumstances. Once a saver's myRA reaches $15,000, or after 30 years, the balance will be rolled over to a private-sector retirement account.

I must admit that the myRA $15,000 savings cap is a drop in the bucket when it comes to actual retirement account balances. But on the other hand, right now, today, how many people do you know that don't have $15,000 in cash or investments? The myRA account is not designed to stop the bleeding, it is offering a band-aid to help heal empty savings accounts through automatic payroll contributions.

Be sure to do your own research on myRA to determine if it will be a good option for you. The goal is to start or resume saving for retirement as soon as possible.

Retirement Planning-What Do You Need to Get Started?

Wealth building for retirement involves short-term, intermediate, and long-term planning. Being as debt free as possible upon your retirement will lower your outgoing expenses. There are ways you can build a much-needed retirement nest egg that will provide you with some financial assistance. Debt is a major reason why people of retirement age do not retire. Wouldn't it be nice to retire debt free, knowing you have the right amount of financial resources coming in that will meet all of your monthly financial needs without taking on a full or part-time job?

Before you begin to plan, you must first understand your goals and needs for retirement. A financial planner can help you. Here are some questions you must be prepared to answer about how your life may change after retirement:

- When will be the right time for me to retire?
- How much money will I need for living expenses? Be sure to factor in inflation.
- When I do retire, will I have enough income so I don't have to work part time?
- Am I scared to retire because I fear I might not live long after?
- Will I outlive my retirement income?
- Am I looking forward to retirement?
- What will I do to occupy my time?
- Where will I live during retirement?
- Will I make new friends during retirement?
- Must I sell my home when I retire?
- Where will my retirement income come from? Social Security, pension, personal savings, IRA/401k, passive real estate income, etc., or will I need financial assistance from friends or family?

Once you have the answers to the questions above, you should be able to begin the retirement planning process. The need for self-education when it comes to you and your retirement is a must. There are several different things you can do that will improve your retirement planning process. Here is a short list to help you get started:

- Reduce or eliminate your debt – reread Chapter 2-Debt Management.
- Estimate your income needs based on your current lifestyle to determine how much money you will need to live on during your retirement years. Do not forget about inflation. Remember to estimate the difference from today's cost of living compared to tomorrows cost.
- Start saving now. Decide how much you can save (e.g. 10% to 20% of your total income). But start with whatever you can. Something is better than nothing. Set up an automatic investment plan through payroll or checking account deductions.
- Increase your retirement plan contributions as often as possible.
- Leave your retirement accounts alone so your money can grow (e.g. no withdrawals or loans from your 401k, 457, etc.). Wait until you are 59 ½ to avoid paying a 10% early withdrawal penalty.
- Stick with your plan, revise your plan when necessary, and review your plan regularly.

Please take your retirement planning seriously so that you will have sufficient funds in your nest egg. You can truly make your retirement years become your golden years. It is your responsibility and yours alone to undertake this task.

No one will have your best personal interests in mind better than you. Do you want to waste a few more years and do nothing by saying to yourself, "I am still young? I have plenty of time to save and invest for retirement…someday." Then all of a sudden ten years have passed and guess what, you still have no retirement savings or investments because you did not take action. It is never too late to start as long as you are alive, you always have the opportunity to save, invest, grow your money, and plan for retirement.

Remember, I said that retirement is based on <u>money,</u> not age. Collecting Social Security is based on age or disability. My wife and I were not old enough to collect Social Security, but we were able to retire at an early age as planned. So, if you had enough wealth regardless of your age to live on for the remainder of your life, you can retire and live financially free at any time. A sound retirement plan can make this a reality.

ESTATE PLANNING

Three things are certain in life: Birth, Taxes, and Death. With the proper estate plan, you can actually have the last say after death and pay Uncle Sam as few death taxes as possible on the estate in which you leave behind. To put it simply, your estate is everything you own. All estates are different in size and its value is determined by your net worth. But no matter how big or small your estate is you should have a plan.

Many of today's millionaires and billionaires have a trust fund (old money) and/or benefited from the proceeds of an estate plan. My point is that someone in their family must have taken estate planning seriously to ensure their hard-earned wealth was passed on.

Estate planning is a tool that is designed to protect your assets, and have your final instructions carried out when you pass on from this earthly life. Or, if one day you are not of sound mind and in good health, and can no longer make decisions for yourself.

If you were to pass on suddenly, by having an estate plan, your family members would not have to make significant decisions in their difficult time of mourning your loss. This can prevent your property from going to probate court where anything could happen.

Estate planning is a process of outlining and identifying your assets along with how you want them to be distributed. Also, estate planning can assist you in ways to minimize estate taxes as much as possible. Estate planning can also put in place a system (proper insurance) to pay off most if not all of any debt that you leave behind. This will ensure that your family members won't bear the hardship of your debt.

Have you inherited something of great value from your parents, grandparents, or another family member? They left you a family heirloom such as real estate, a business, jewelry, property, stocks, bonds or even cash. Someone wanted to pass something on to the next generation to ensure the family name and assets will remain in the family many years after they have passed on. It is now your obligation to carry the torch that has been lit by an elder and passed on to you.

Your estate should have some legal structure for protection. Your estate plan can be contested in court by family members, but if your documents are in proper order, your wishes most likely will be carried out.

Actually, everyone already has an estate plan. It has been created by the laws of the state and/or city in which you live. Without having your own official written, documented estate plan, the state will speak for you. If you have a plan, you can speak for yourself. This is a very serious matter and you should be well aware of what might happen to your family and assets if you pass on from this life without an official, sound, legally documented plan.

Think about your spouse if you are married, and consider the following generations to come. What do you have in place that would ensure the family estate would remain in the family? You might want a long-time special friend to have some jewelry or charitable organization to get a cash donation. Whatever it is, put it in writing.

One of the most important decisions you will need to make is to determine who will be responsible for carrying out your wishes. You will need to appoint an executor and co-executor and possibly a trustee (someone who manages the trust) and a guardian (if you leave dependents) for your estate. The executor is responsible for passing on your assets the way you requested. You can name a family member. You can also have an executor who is a non-family member to carry out your instructions. A co-executor should be named just in case the primary executor is unavailable to perform his or her duties.

Here are some different elements (but not limited to) that can make up an estate plan:

- revocable or irrevocable last will and testament
- revocable or irrevocable living trust agreement
- revocable or irrevocable living will
- health care directive
- land trust
- insurance trust
- durable power of attorney

There are some do-it-yourself kits you can purchase from bookstores or online for a fraction of the cost of having a professional planner outline these important tasks. If you understand the legal terminology and you know what is needed to complete all the necessary paperwork, by all means give it your best shot. If you want the work to be performed by an estate planning professional, then spend the time to research the professionals of your choice. They have the expert knowledge to give you the best chance of protecting your estate. Only then should you take the necessary steps to go through the estate planning process.

The assets protected by estate planning can be passed on from one generation to another. Remember your estate is everything you own even if some things don't have an actual financial value. As long as it has value to you, it is part of your estate. If handled responsibly, your estate could grow from thousands of dollars to millions of dollars, even billions over time. And, if your estate has any value, you should consult with an experienced estate tax specialist and strategist to ensure you don't also leave an enormous tax burden on your family.

Estate Planning–Getting Started

I suggested before that you can retain the services of the estate planner. First and foremost, do your research on that person or company. Someone who is recommended by word of mouth often reduces your risk, but there is no substitute for research. Use the same care that allowed you to select your financial planner. Once you have decided on the right person to meet your needs, make sure the cost of their services is reasonable. Have a clear and easy to read written cost agreement. It will not hurt to do a cost comparison of about three or four different estate planners so you can get a price range that should help you make the best choice.

You and the planner should agree upon a time and place to meet. The planner might suggest meeting at your home or office. I recommend the office visit, for the same reasons as I outlined in the Financial Planning section.

Good planners are flexible and will advise you of your options. Some things you will need to consider when you first get started with your estate planning session include but are not limited to:

- A list and location of all assets including in-state and out-of-state real estate, cars, boats, furs, jewelry, cash, gold, diamonds, etc., and who owns each asset.
- A list of all liabilities with creditor contact information, due dates, and total amounts due.
- A list of all beneficiary names and contact information.
- Copies of important documents such as divorce decree, adoption, separation, marriage licenses, deeds, and titles.
- Your employee benefits plan identification number, contact information, and balances for pension, 401k or 457 plans, etc.
- Account numbers and balances such as credit union, CDs, checking, savings and IRA`s and annuities.
- Contact information for executors, trustees, and/or guardians.

This is a sample starter list that you can review to help you gather some of the necessary information needed. Once you have your first meeting with your estate planner, they will provide further guidance as to the exact documentation needed.

It is also a good idea to be candid in your family discussions concerning who your inheritors are and what it is you want them to have. So there would be no need for family members to have to work things out on their own when it comes to your wishes. By having your final wishes in writing, family members will know exactly what you want to take place.

Once completed, a good estate plan should consist of at least four key elements:

1. Financial planning is to ensure you have enough money to live on until you pass on from this life as we know it.
2. Inheritance planning allows you to decide while you are still alive and in sound health and mind, who gets your money, property, and personal possessions.
3. Tax planning helps you to prevent the government from taking most if not all of your money for taxes - while you are alive, and after you pass on.
4. Insurance planning can provide financial and health-related assistance for you and your heirs depending upon the situation and coverage. Life insurance is a good tax-free way to leave cash to your family.

You have spent your life working hard to be successful and provide a future for you and your family. For you to get to where you are today, you had to make many different decisions. Some of the decisions were good and some were not. But you made decisions anyway because it was required. Now you have another critical decision to make. Should your success end after you pass on from this life? NO!

You have the chance while you are alive to reach back and extend a helping hand to your family members and let them know that your hard work and success gave them a chance to enhance the quality of their life for many generations to come.

You can be the first person in your family to break a cycle of not passing assets on to future generations. An estate plan eliminates most if not all of the challenges your estate might face if you die Intestate (i.e. dying without having a written will). It can help your estate avoid probate court and allows you to give to your worthy heirs or shut down uncooperative ones. Only you can protect your legacy.

TAX PLANNING

The 16th Amendment to the United States Constitution states in part: "The Congress shall have the power to lay and collect taxes on incomes from whatever source derived."

Your tax planning needs should include how to legally minimize the amount of taxes you pay while living, as well as the amount your estate could pay after death.

The government takes this amendment very seriously. Tax revenue is used by the government to pay for services that help the country function. There are many different taxes one might pay due to Federal, State, and local tax codes.

For those of you newly entered or preparing to enter the workforce, you will experience first paycheck shock! You may have started out working part-time/below minimum wage jobs such as babysitting, cutting grass, or stocking shelves at the corner store. These jobs usually paid you in cash so you received the full amount of your pay; e.g. $5.00 per hour for 40 hours of work, you got $200.00.

However, you now have a new job that pays at least the minimum wage. Let's use Chicago's minimum wage of $10.00 per hour as of July 2015. When you received your first official paycheck for 40 hours of work, you discovered you did not/ will not get the full $400.00. It was closer to the $200.00 you got from your non-minimum wage job. "Why", might you ask?

This happened because there were and will continue to be mandatory and/or voluntary deductions taken from your $400.00 (i.e. Gross Pay) each pay period. Your paystub will contain all of the deductions used to compute your Net Pay = (Gross Pay − Deductions):

Mandatory Deductions

The main and largest deductions are employment related taxes:

- Federal income tax withholding − to fund the government

- State and/or City income tax withholding – to fund the local government
- FICA – to fund Social Security
- Medicare – to fund senior/disabled health insurance

Note: Union dues, insurance and retirement savings are other voluntary deductions that may be taken if you sign up for them

As you continue through life, some of the other taxes you might encounter include but are not limited to the following:

- inheritance/estate
- property (see Real Estate chapter on how to possibly lower property taxes)
- sales
- early withdrawal penalty (before 59 ½ years of age) from retirement funds
- and much more

The Internal Revenue Service (IRS) is the government agency assigned to the duty of collecting all Federal taxes. Income taxes are a primary source of revenue for Federal, State and local governments. To ensure most citizens pay their share, taxes are withheld (i.e. pre-paid) from your payroll check. You can decide on the amount of taxes that should be withheld, or request tax exempt status for a select period of time on your Employee Withholding Allowance Certificate (W-4). You will received a W-4 when you first start working but you can make changes anytime throughout the year. Regardless of your choice, you are still required to pay Uncle Sam his taxes. If you are a business owner, you are required to pay estimated taxes during the year.

Depending upon how much tax was withheld, you may get a refund from the IRS. If you did not pay enough taxes throughout the year, you might owe Uncle Sam (IRS). If you owe additional taxes, you may want to decrease your W-4 payroll exemptions or increase your estimated business payments so they can withhold more money.

If you are getting large refunds, you are actually giving the government an interest-free loan until you file your taxes. Why let the government continue to benefit from your hard work? Review (increase) your W-4 payroll withholding exemptions/estimated payments and ensure you are only paying the minimum needed to cover your tax liability. You can take the additional cash flow and add it your Debt Elimination Rollover Payment Plan. If you are already out of debt, you can start or increase saving or investing.

Also, look into tax-exempt investments, before-tax retirement contributions, gift giving and other ways to minimize the amount of taxes you are required to pay.

It is a financial kiss of death while you are on the road to building wealth, not to pay attention to your taxes. If you owe, Uncle Sam says, "pay me now (tax due date or extension due date) or pay me more later, but pay you shall"! If you owe taxes, why not pay them to avoid additional penalties which will eat up more of your business profits or hard earned W-2 (Employee Annual Wage and Withholding Form) employee wage income.

Depending on the type of tax you are required to pay, there are different deadlines throughout the year that are imposed. The IRS requires you to complete your personal and business income tax returns by these deadlines. Be sure to check the tax authority websites for these dates.

If you are savvy enough to understand the IRS tax code, then do your own taxes. If you need assistance, a Financial Planner or Tax Accountant can be a big help in this area. But by all means obtain professional consultation to best address both your personal and business tax concerns.

ASSET INSURANCE PLANNING

What if something beyond your control happened, like a natural disaster or a freak accident? You might lose your life, your most personal and precious possessions, your automobile, heirlooms, home, etc. What would you do? How would you replace all of your lost possessions? No amount of insurance can replace the loss of life, but it can help take care of your family. There is a safety net or security blanket called, "insurance." Insurance allows you to have some kind of financial relief if you have the proper coverage from a reputable insurance provider.

There are many types of insurance to consider for your portfolio:

- whole life – pays a benefit upon death and/or can provide lifetime income for the policyholder
- term Life – pays a benefit if the policyholder dies within a specified time and/or age limit
- medical, dental, and vision
- long term care provides nursing-home care, home health care, personal or adult day care usually for age 65 or older or persons with chronic or disabling conditions who need constant supervision
- auto liability at a minimum but also comprehensive to cover your vehicle.
- homeowners
- umbrella liability - designed to give added liability protection above and beyond the limits on other policies such as homeowners and auto
- renters, personal property replacement

Your insurance portfolio is (or should be) a plan of action put in place that will offer you financial or health assistance in your time of need. When you pass on from life, do you have the proper amount of life insurance that will cover your burial needs? Social Security pays a death benefit of $255.00. With no insurance or cash reserve, that alone is not enough.

Funerals cost several thousand dollars. It is a nice feeling to know that when the time comes, you will have the financial means to lay you or your loved one(s) to rest in a respectable manner. Also, will you have the proper amount of available insurance that would also help pay the remainder of your expenses? Will it allow your family to keep the house, pay off debts or go to college? These are some things you need to consider when determining how much insurance to purchase.

What about auto insurance? What would happen if you were involved in an accident that was or was not your fault?

Operating a motor vehicle without insurance is illegal. Will your current auto insurance cover the damages as well as possible hospital bills and time off from work?

Health (you are your biggest asset) insurance could be considered the most important of all insurance coverage. Does your health insurance provider pay you while you are laid up in the hospital? Do you have medical, dental, and vision care? Do you have any kind of long-term health care coverage?

Health insurance can assist in maintaining your quality of life. With bad health, you can lose everything that you own but with proper medical care you can regain your health- (See Chapter 8-Health Planning for more details).

To receive the benefits that your insurance contract offers, you should be current with all terms of agreement when your time of need arises to help avoid additional hardships.

You should meet with an insurance specialist or your financial planner and take the necessary steps to ensure adequate protection of your valuable assets. (See Appendix for insurance company rating services contact information).

Summary

Are you comfortable with your current financial plan? Is there a need to start or restructure your current plan? What if you lost your current job and had to take a minimum wage paying job? Would you be physically and financially ready to make the change? During the recession and the government shut down, people were downsizing all across the country because of loss of income. If something was to, unfortunately, happen to you beyond your control, and you were no longer of sound mind, what would happen? Who would take charge? What would happen to your spouse, children and personal property? All of the many different areas of planning are important. STOP PROCRASTINATING! Make your financial action plans today!
REMEMBER "THE BEST IMPROVEMENT STARTS WITH SELF IMPROVEMENT."

POEM - IF YOU

If you self-educate without any haste

Your mind will not be a terrible waste

If you need to seek help

I hope that you do

Dig deep down inside for that special clue

If you fail to plan, you plan to fail

That`s like touching the financial third rail

If you have a plan, it will show you the way

Helping guarantee things will turn out ok

If you write down your plans, then work them out

You will feel better, without a doubt

If you believe in your plans, then work and do

Success one day will come true for you

-MICHAEL "BART" MATHEWS

CHAPTER 8
HEALTH & WELLNESS PLANNING

"An ounce of prevention is worth a pound of cure."

-BEN FRANKLIN

W HICH ONE DO you think is more important, your health, or your wealth? What is the point of having wealth if you are not healthy (mentally, physically, spiritually and emotionally) enough to enjoy it and help others in need? It should be clear that your health and wellness should be the most important factor. Without good health and wellness, it will be hard for you to fully enjoy whatever wealth you might acquire.

How many times have you or someone you know called on the Lord to take away their pain and suffering while lying in a hospital bed? How many times have you prayed for someone who needed a divine intervention because the medical doctors said they could do no more? My point is, the spiritual and mental aspect of health and wellness are just as important (I think so) as the physical aspect.

So what is health planning? It is putting into motion a plan of action that will assist in helping you maintain a healthy quality of life. Depending on your particular health situation, all the wealth in the world might not be able to save you. Whether it is your physical, mental, spiritual or financial health, you must do your due diligence in turning yourself into the best overall person that you can possibly be.

Health and wellness planning should include the following, but not limited to;

- Establishing health insurance (see Affordable Care Act below), give your health insurance companies name, telephone number and account number to your trusted family member in case of emergency.
- Make healthier food choices include lots of fruits and vegetables.
- Get regular physicals, ask questions about your health.
- Establish a 30 to 60-minute exercise routine after consultation and approval by your doctor.
- Minimize your alcohol consumption or just don't drink.
- Don't take illegal drugs.
- Don't overtake prescription medication, don't give or sell your prescription medicine to anyone!
- No smoking.
- Minimize your sodium (salt) and sugar (e.g. soda pop) intake.
- Drink plenty of water.
- Practice safe sex - use protection (condoms) to help prevent unwanted pregnancies and spreading Sexually Transmitted Diseases (STD). Making the wrong sexual choice can have harsh consequences for your future as well as adding additional burden on your family!
- Sleep 7 to 8 hours per night, keep a regular sleep cycle.
- Keep copies of your medical records (paper, CD or USB stick), the more information available to health care providers the better, some examples are;

  o   contact information for your health care provider
  o   types of illnesses

o   medications and prescriptions
o   medical alerts (include allergies)
o   family medical history

EXERCISE IS VITAL TO YOUR HEALTH

Exercise and healthy eating have always been considered an important factor in maintaining health and wellness. Your doctor should always be consulted before starting any form of exercise to ensure you don't injure yourself.

Many join health clubs, hire personal trainers while others exercise at home using workout or training videos on their own.

Walking is a natural form of exercise for people of all ages who want to lose weight or improve their health and wellness. A vast majority of health and fitness experts suggest that walking 10,000 steps per day or exercising 30-60 minutes per day will have a significant effect on your long-lasting weight loss and overall health and wellness.

Walking 10,000 steps per day has been suggested to help in reducing the risk of heart disease, plaque buildup in your arteries, stroke or heart attack. Walking helps to reduce and manage your blood pressure. Lowering the risk of having diabetes is another health advantage. The faster you walk, the more calories your body burns, now add changing your eating habits and you will begin to see results over time.

Here are several suggestions that will enable you to add thousands of steps beyond your day to day regular walking routine. Using a pedometer will assist you in tracking the number of steps and calories burned. Even your phone, watch and other wearable gadgets can track the number of calories burned, distance walked and the number of steps taken during your entire day. They can also monitor your sleep habits. You might be surprised at how easy you can add more steps than you first anticipated. Most importantly, being a couch potato will net you ZERO benefits:

- Drive less, walk more.
- When driving is a must, park as far and safely away from the entry way door of your destination, only during daylight hours.

- When using public transportation (bus/train/taxi) exit the vehicle several blocks before your destination and walk the remainder of the way.
- Walk instead of using escalator's or elevators at work or elsewhere.
- Walk at a fast pace during lunch at least 10 minutes adding approx. 1,000 steps to your daily count.
- Go dancing and or take up a dance class.
- Get the family involved! Walk the children to the playground and let them burn off calories playing with friends while you are adding to your 10,000 steps per day.
- Participate in a team sport that requires foot movement (if you are healthy enough to do so).
- Mall walk; winter and summer time mall walking is free and keeps you out of the elements during inclement weather. Remember, you are going to the mall to walk, not to charge up your credit card and get into debt!
- Purchase a new or used treadmill or stationary bike for your home.

EAT HEALTHY

Exercise alone is not enough. Changing your diet to start eating healthier is required to improve your health and wellness. A good balance of both exercise and healthy eating can go a long way towards reaching your wellness goals. Billions are spent each year on exercise equipment, fitness center memberships, personal trainers, plastic surgery, liposuction and weight loss diets to improve our lives and appearance.

There are numerous diet (wellness) programs that are advertised via the media. Each of these programs has different approaches to eating healthy and losing weight. You should research all diets and consult your doctor before following any particular one.

However, according to President Obama's Council on Fitness, Sports, and Nutrition website (www.fitness.gov), it's easier than you think to start eating healthy. Making small changes to your eating habits each week can improve your nutritional health, just like making small changes to reduce your debts/expenses, can improve your financial health. They offer eight healthy eating goals to incorporate into your diet:

1. Make half your plate fruits and vegetables.
2. Make half the grains you eat whole grains.
3. Switch to fat-free or low-fat (1%) milk.
4. Choose a variety of lean protein foods.
5. Compare sodium in foods.
6. Drink water instead of sugary drinks.
7. Eat some seafood (if you are not allergic).
8. Cut back on solid fats.

Exercising and eating healthy applies to all members of your family, especially your children. Just as you should teach them financial literacy, you should also teach them how to live a healthy lifestyle. Make healthy living a family affair. Involve the children in choosing healthy food while grocery shopping as well as how to cook more healthy.

Another initiative supported by President Obama's Council is "Let's Move!" Let's Move! is a comprehensive initiative, launched by First Lady Michelle Obama, dedicated to solving the problem of childhood obesity within a generation. So that kids born today will grow up healthier and be able to pursue their dreams. This is an ambitious goal, but it can be done. The President's Council supports "Let's Move!" through outreach, events, and partnerships. You can check the website (www.fitness.gov) for more information on all of the government's health and wellness programs.

Health and wellness planning and practice is a must and should not be ignored. Lead by example. The life you save might be your own, a family member or friend!

THE IMPORTANCE OF HEALTH INSURANCE

Health insurance is the best way to protect your most precious assets – You and your family. It is also the best way to pay for your health needs because it has been proven that certain disabilities or other health related issues can wipe out your entire life savings.

If this happens, you are now penniless and you still have bad health in addition to now having no wealth. Your situation might be irreversible and require you to have ongoing care at home, or in a nursing home. With the soaring cost of prescription drugs along with other ongoing health and wellness issues, you need health insurance.

Types of items health insurance include, but not limited to:

- annual physicals and wellness visits
- medical emergency
- dental
- vision
- short term disability
- long term care
- prescription drugs
- physical therapy
- mental health services
- medical devices

The Affordable Care Act

According to the website (www.medicaid.gov), the Affordable Care Act (aka Obamacare) was passed in March of 2010. The Affordable Care Act actually refers to two separate pieces of legislation — the Patient Protection and Affordable Care Act (P.L. 111-148) and the Health Care and Education Reconciliation Act of 2010 (P.L. 111-152). Together they expand Medicaid coverage to millions of low-income Americans and make numerous improvements to both Medicaid and the Children Health Insurance Program (CHIP).

Because of this piece of legislation more Americans now have access to health care than ever before. Several major features of the Affordable Care Act consist of:

- Mandating that all U.S. citizens get health insurance coverage – income tax penalties will be assessed for failure to get coverage.
- Providing health insurance subsidies for low-income households.
- Eliminating pre-existing conditions that prevent you and your dependents from getting health insurance.
- Requiring insurers to include prevention and long-term care medical services within their basic coverage plans.

You must meet certain eligibility requirements to apply for health care under the Affordable Care Act:

- You must live in the United States of America.
- You must be an American citizen.
- Must not be in jail at the time you apply for insurance.
- U.S. citizens living abroad or in U.S. territories are not required to get health insurance under the Affordable Care Act.

You can apply for health insurance online via the website (www.healthcare.gov) or place a call (1.800.318.2596) to the Health Insurance Marketplace (aka health insurance exchange). The Marketplace helps uninsured people find health insurance coverage.

If you go online to the website (www.healthcare.gov) or your state Marketplace, you will be able to browse plans in your state before applying. You can fill out the Marketplace application online. After you complete the application, the Marketplace will tell you if you qualify for:

- Private health insurance plans which cover essential health benefits, pre-existing conditions and preventive care.
- Lower monthly premiums based upon your household size and income.
- Medicaid and the Children's Health Insurance Program (CHIP) – these programs cover millions of low/limited income families.

If you call they will mail you an application that you can complete and send back to them or they can help you apply over the phone.

If you are covered by an employer-sponsored plan, you don't need to go to the Marketplace. If you are married and your spouse is on and can remain on your employer-provided insurance plan, your spouse does not need to sign up under the Affordable Care Act.

If they are not covered by your employer plan, they will need to get covered via the Marketplace or other private insurance options. To find a private insurance provider (e.g. health, vision, dental), you may want to contact A.M. Best Company or Moody's to find and compare insurance company's ratings. (See Appendix for insurance company rating services contact information).

When selecting a health care plan whether through the Affordable Care Act, employer-sponsored or private insurance, you need to know exactly what coverage(s) the plan includes. They should include health, dental, vision, hearing and/or prescription drugs to ensure your basic needs will be covered. Consider other factors too, such as low or no co-pay for office visits, available physician and specialist access.

Be sure to obtain the health insurance plan(s) that offers the best overall health care benefits that work best for you and your family and budget. The Affordable Care Act just expanded the opportunity for all Americans to obtain health care. It's the law.

Family Medical Leave Act (FMLA) allows employees unpaid time off work to care for themselves or family members who are seriously ill without losing their job. Knowing you have approved time off is an important benefit that will add to the quality of life in times of health-related needs.

PHYSICALS-CAN BE LIFE-SAVING

If you have health care insurance and pay a premium and you do not see a doctor regularly, you are wasting your money as well as putting your health in jeopardy. As part of the Affordable Care Act, all insurance plans must include coverage for annual physicals. Many people visit a doctor only when something serious happens. Don't you be that person! Call your doctor, schedule an appointment and get a physical now!

Just for the record, I get a physical every year. My check-up includes a prostate check, blood work, ear, nose and throat check, body temperature, blood pressure and heart check among other tests. I just want to let you know, I practice what I preach!

Just like you take your vehicle to the dealer for that 3,000-mile oil change and mechanical checkup, you should take your body to a physician for a medical checkup! What happens to your car if you never keep up with the service schedule? Sooner or later it starts to break down and parts need to be replaced.

The same is true with the human body. If you do not take care of it, it will not take care of you. Your time and the quality of life will be vastly improved if you consider your health and wellness to be your most valuable asset, so protect it.

THE DEADLY KILLERS

Physicals can also help to discover three of the most prevalent deadly killers: cancer, heart disease, and diabetes. Stroke is another serious condition that is affecting thousands of Americans each day. If you want to know your risk of getting these diseases, it is your responsibility to make the necessary appointment with your health care provider. Make sure your doctor tests for these conditions during your regular physical, or more frequently if you have a family history of these diseases.

Early detection and treatment are the keys to surviving these diseases. Today it seems like we all know someone that has been affected by one or more of these illnesses. Below is a brief description of each of these killers. High blood pressure and bad cholesterol have also been determined to be contributing factors to declining health.

Cancer

Cancer is the abnormal and uncontrolled malignant growth of cells that attack major parts of the body. It can spread rapidly to other areas of the body and can lead to death if left untreated.

My Personal Experience with Cancer

My passion for cancer prevention comes from my own experience with two family members who suffered different forms of cancer. One family member is currently a cervical cancer survivor. Because she had regular physicals, she was diagnosed early and treated, resulting in a full recovery. She is here with us today.

Another family member, who did not get regular checkups, was diagnosed with Stage 4 lung cancer in April of 2006. She underwent chemotherapy as well as prescription drug therapy. In October of 2006, she lost her battle with cancer and passed on from this life.

Despite all the modern marvels of today's medicine, she was in constant pain; her hair completely fell out, and she was virtually unable to move. I do not write about my family members as a bid for sympathy, but to bring to light the ongoing need for early cancer detection and prevention.

Cancer may affect you, a loved one or friend during your lifetime. If it does, my hope is that you are aware of the many challenges that might be ahead. Had my relative with stage 4 lung cancer not smoked for the many years that she did and had she gone to the doctor for regular physicals, early detection might have prolonged her life.

It is true that non-smokers can also develop lung cancer and die, just the same as a smoker. But if you do not smoke and take annual physicals, your life expectancy might be significantly prolonged.

Below is a list of the most prevalent cancers. Other than prostrate, these diseases can affect both male and female.

Lung Cancer

Lung cancer is said to be the deadliest of all cancers. There are four stages of lung cancer – 1 to 4 which indicates how far the cancer has spread.

If you smoke, chances are you might develop lung cancer faster than a non-smoker. Second-hand smoke is also said to be a prime contributor to lung cancer.

If you don't smoke, don't start. If you do smoke, quit now! Seek information on cessation programs that can help you quit smoking.

Breast Cancer

This cancer usually occurs in women, but in some cases men also develop breast cancer. There are five stages of breast cancer. There is stage 0 which is non-invasive. Invasive breast cancer stages range from 1 to 4. Treatment for breast cancer can consist of one or more of the following: surgery, chemotherapy, and radiation. There are also holistic treatments options as well.

Breast cancer can be treated successfully if detected early. There are various ways to detect breast cancer:

- mammogram
- ultrasound
- clinical breast examination
- self-breast examination

Cervical Cancer

Cervical cancer is a malignant tumor which starts in the cells of the lining of the cervix. Normal cells gradually develop pre-cancerous changes that turn into cancer. The primary method for detecting cervical cancer is during a pap-smear. A yearly pap smear should be included with your annual physical.

Prostate Cancer

Prostate cancer is only applicable to men. It is the most common type of cancer diagnosed in American men and is more common in African-American men versus any other race of people. The normal age to begin your prostate cancer screening is age 50 for the average American male. It is suggested that because of the high risk of prostate cancer in the African-American community, 40 years is the recommended age to begin screening.

The prostate exam during your regular physical checkup consists of taking a blood test to get a PSA level as well as a manual rectal exam. The most common way is for the doctor to instruct the patient to bend over the table, lean forward on both elbows allowing the doctor to insert his/her finger into the rectum and examine the prostate.

Depending upon a combination of your PSA level, your age and the condition of your prostate (soft is healthy, firm or hard usually requires more testing), you may need to undergo additional tests to determine if you actually have Prostate Cancer. A prostate biopsy may be required if more advanced testing is recommended by your doctor, as was the case with me. Happily my results were negative!

A PSA level greater than 3 may be a cause of concern so be sure to monitor and track your PSA levels every year to determine if it is going up. Consult your doctor and do your research on a reputable medical site to ensure you fully understand what your PSA levels means and any associated risks for prostate cancer.

Colon and Rectum (Colorectal) Cancer

The colon and rectum are parts of the digestive system. Together they form a large muscular tube called the large intestine. Starting at age 50, men and women who are deemed to be at average risk for colorectal cancer should begin routine tests. Some various ways of detections are:

- A fecal occult blood test or F.O.B.T. once a year.
- A sigmoidoscopy every five years.
- A colonoscopy every ten years after age 50, if low risk.
- A double-contrast barium enema every 5 to 10 years.
- A digital rectal exam every 5 to 10 years.

My wife and I are grateful to have had our first colonoscopy many years ago. The test was done by licensed medical doctors in a hospital setting. We both received a clean bill of health.

Diabetes

According to the American Diabetes Association, "Diabetes is a disease in which the body does not produce or properly use insulin." Insulin is a hormone that is needed to convert sugar, starches, and other food into energy needed for daily life. The cause of diabetes continues to be a mystery, although both genetics and environmental factors such as obesity and lack of exercise are considered to be major contributing factors. If detected early and treated, diabetes can be successfully managed in most cases.

Four major types of Diabetes are:

- type 1
- type 2
- gestational diabetes
- pre-diabetes

Consult your health care provider for more detailed information on Diabetes, its symptoms, causes, and treatment options.

Heart Disease

According to the American Heart Association, many risk factors can contribute to heart disease. Heart disease can possibility lead to a heart attack. Some of the risks factors are manageable and some are not:

- your age
- your genetics or family history
- obesity and, unhealthy eating
- high cholesterol
- hardening of the arteries

Heart Attack Warning Signs

Some heart attacks are sudden and intense. But most heart attacks start slowly, with mild pain or discomfort. Often people affected aren't sure what's wrong and wait too long before getting help. Here are signs that can mean a heart attack may be happening:

- **Chest discomfort-**most heart attacks involve some discomfort in the center of the chest that lasts more than a few minutes, or that goes away and comes back. It can feel like heartburn, uncomfortable pressure, squeezing, fullness or pain.
- **Discomfort in other areas of the upper body-**symptoms can include pain or discomfort in one or both arms, the back, neck, jaw or stomach.
- **Shortness of breath-**with or without chest discomfort.
- Other signs may include breaking out in a cold sweat, nausea or lightheadedness.

As with men, women's most common heart attack symptom is chest pain or discomfort. But women are somewhat more likely than men to experience some of the other common symptoms, particularly shortness of breath, nausea/vomiting, and back or jaw pain.

The Warning Signs of Stroke

According to the National Stroke Association (www. stroke.org), a stroke happens about every 40 seconds. Each year, about 795,000 Americans have a stroke. Do you know the warning signs? If you do have stroke warning signs, this means your brain isn't getting the blood it needs. Damage may be temporary or permanent. For example, you might lose the ability to speak but recover with time. You might have a partial or complete weakness, in an arm or leg.

Over time, symptoms of a stroke develop gradually depending upon the type of stroke, where it occurs in the brain, and how severe it is. But if you are having a stroke, you are more likely to have one or more sudden warning signs like these:

- numbness or weakness in your face, arm, or leg, especially on one side
- confusion or trouble understanding other people
- trouble speaking
- trouble seeing with one or both eyes
- trouble walking or staying balanced or coordinated

- dizziness
- a severe headache that occurs for no known reason

"The most important thing to do if stroke symptoms appear is to **"Think FAST"** as follows:

- **Face** - Ask the person to smile. Does one side of the face droop?
- **Arms** - Ask the person to raise both arms. Does one arm drift downward? Or is one arm unable to raise up?
- **Speech** - Ask the person to repeat a simple phrase. Is his or her speech slurred or strange?
- **Time** - If you observe any of these signs, call 911 or your local emergency number immediately. Don't wait to see if the symptoms go away.

Every minute counts. The longer a stroke goes untreated, the greater the potential for brain damage and disability. If you're with someone you suspect is having a stroke, watch the person carefully while waiting for emergency assistance so you can tell emergency personnel your observations.

Summary

The government has made the health and wellness of all Americans a priority. They have mandated health insurance for all citizens. If you have insurance, use it. If you do not have insurance, get some. If you cannot afford health insurance, seek government assistance. Put your pride aside because the life you save just might be your own or your family member.

They have initiated programs to provide tips about healthy eating, obesity and exercising. Eating healthy and staying active is a lifestyle choice you should consider for yourself and your family. For best results consult your physician, registered nurse, dietitian or certified personal trainer for guidance.

The Cancer Research and Prevention Foundation have encouraged people to learn how to reduce the risk of getting cancer through a healthy lifestyle and regular screening tests. If you smoke, QUIT!

The American Diabetes and the American Heart Association both encourages the best possible lifestyle to help prevent diabetes, heart attacks, and strokes. There are options for a greater chance of survival with research, self-education and action. (See Appendix for medical information resources).

Remember, good health is the cornerstone of all success. No amount of wealth is important as good health. One day we all will leave this earth, some sooner than others because of lack of regular health care. You have the power to prolong your life, in some cases. You just have to plan to live longer, healthier and wealthier.

REMEMBER,"THE BEST IMPROVEMENT STARTS WITH SELF IMPROVEMENT"

POEM - HEALTHY LIVING

If you want to lose weight, this is a clue

Better health and wellness, is just right for you

Unhealthy eating, it`s time to cease

Eat smaller portions, cut down on the feast

Exercise daily, 30 minutes or more

Make it fun, and not a chore

Walk around the track, strengthen your core

Take line dancing lessons, on the studio floor

Enjoy a long ride, on the bicycle trail

Dropping more weight, now excited to tell

Eat more fruits and veggies, cut down on bad fat

You're dropping more weight, now how about that

Carrots, broccoli, celery, and beans

You can also eat some turnip greens

Oranges, strawberries, pears, and grapefruit

Keep this up, looking good in your suit

Mix up a smoothie, enjoy the fresh taste

Continue exercising without any haste

Health and wellness are not a joke

It lessens the chances of you having a stroke!

-Michael Bart Mathews

CHAPTER 9
THE CHILDREN ARE OUR FUTURE

"Children are our greatest treasure. They are our future."

-Nelson Mandela

A s THEY WERE growing up, I always talked to my grandchildren about financial literacy. They always heard me say, "the choices you make with your money today can help you live a better life tomorrow." When they did earn money for small odd jobs, I asked them, how much are you going to save before you start spending? I've tried to instill in them to make paying themselves first a habit at an early age.

To change or help prevent some of the past financial mistakes of adults, it is important to teach our children money management and wealth building principles at an early age. Financial literacy education is just as important for children as reading and writing.

According to an international survey conducted by PISA, 18 percent of American 15-year-olds surveyed, could not answer basic financial questions or handle simple tasks, like understanding an invoice. The Program for International Student Assessment (PISA) is a worldwide study, by the Organization for Economic Co-operation and Development (OECD) in member and non-member nations, of 15-year-old school pupils' scholastic performance on mathematics, science, and reading.

When you give your children money, do you give them instructions on how to manage it other than spending all of it? A simple financial direction like, "be sure to save some of that money" is the first step. Giving them a home piggy bank as a birthday or Christmas present gives them a starting place to save their money.

Once they have enough money, open a savings account for them. Have them accompany you to the bank so they can make all deposits into their own accounts and establish a relationship with their personal banker. Have regular discussions about compounding interest, interest rates, checks, and balances.

You can purchase games based on financial literacy and money management principles that include making transactions with play money from different dominations to help make learning both fun and educational.

Right before my youngest granddaughter turned 6-years of age, I introduced her to the Game of Life. After she had chosen College or Career as her path, she loved to spend the wheel. She was eager to see the number of spaces she could advance her car down the road of her chosen path getting closer to retirement as the end goal.

There were many lessons for her to learn, but I did not want to overwhelm her in the beginning. Her goal was to end up with more money than grandpa! My goal during her game playing time was that she learned financial literacy concepts while having fun with grandpa at the same time. Her favorite part of the game was pay day. She knew that if she passed or landed on a pay day square, she collected her salary from the bank immediately.

Every time she came over she asked to play the Game of Life. She was eager and excited to learn about money while playing. I took the time to teach her while she was in a playful learning mood! She would light up at the end of the game because she was able to count her money (with Grandma's help). I have to admit she won more often than I did! She also wanted to tear the plastic wrapper off of the Monopoly game and jump right in. I will teach her Monopoly and Rich Dad/ Poor Dad Cash Flow games once she masters the Game of Life, which shouldn't take very long.

You should have open discussions with your children and grandchildren concerning the day to day financial transactions needed to keep the household functioning. Have them help you pay the bills from time to time so they can see how much money you have and where the money goes, and most importantly what is actually left over if anything at all.

Talk to them about your job and what type of career they want to pursue. Encourage them to consider learning how to own their own business; becoming entrepreneurs instead of just working a 9-to-5 job.

I was really inspired by a story I heard about John W. Rogers, Jr. At age 12, John's father started buying him dividend-paying stocks for Christmas and his birthday instead of expensive toys. As he grew up, he became very interested in Wall Street. He learned more and more about economics and finance and eventually became a stockbroker. The end result was, he founded Ariel Investments, a multi-billion dollar mutual fund company, at the age of 25.

If you give a person a fish, you feed him for a day. If you teach a person how to fish, you feed him for life. I think John Rogers was taught how to fish. So my wife and I followed John's father's example. We opened savings accounts for all of our grandchildren. Instead of buying them an abundance of material things (toys) for their birthday and Christmas, they now get monetary deposits for these occasions.

The amount of the deposit depends upon their grades and behavior during the year. The better their performance on the job (i.e. school), the more they earn. They also earn a yearly bonus based on how many A's and B's they receive at the end of the school year. Their savings accounts have grown quite a bit.

LESSONS WELL LEARNED

My oldest grandson, Nakii, was age 12 when he asked me to give him $10.00. Before I could say anything, he said he would come over to do some work around the house to earn the money because he did not like asking for a hand-out. He said that he just wanted to earn his keep. He learned the value of earning his money. He is currently in the United States Navy and will be 21-years-old in 2015.

To see how much they have learned and understood about money, I asked all of my grandchildren to write what they felt about money. In the 2007 first edition, our granddaughter Janina, was age 11, when she wrote in her own words what she thought about money.

For this second edition, two more grandchildren added their thoughts; granddaughter Nadia, age 16, was a high school junior and granddaughter Natahlia, age 14, was a high school freshman. Their comments are listed below.

JANINA SPENCER

"I think money should only be spent for good and important causes. I think money should be kept for emergencies. When I grow up and make money in Journalism, I will do many good things with it. I will use my money to buy houses for poor people. I will use my money to get children who are sick and haven't any money to go to a hospital.

I will use my money to buy better supplies for schools. Of course, you are thinking how can I pay for this? I plan to be rich! In my future, I plan to spend my money for good and important things, and things I need. I hope you spend your money wisely". **Reprinted from the 1st edition of Financially Speaking.**

She also wrote the poem below about money titled "Money II." Not bad for an 11-year-old back then. She turned 20-years-old in 2015 and is a sophomore in college with her career goal focused on Film/Movie Production. She has worked hard to earn scholarships to help with the cost of her education. She used the money we saved for her to help fund her school trip to China. She had an "awesome experience." She is off to a great start while realizing her dreams of becoming rich in all areas of her life starting with education.

NADIA TUCKER

I am 15 years old, in the 10th grade living with my mother, father and younger sister Natahlia.

Money is an important asset to the world. It is like the main screw that holds everything together. In my opinion, money is kind of new and modern because it has changed so much.

It began as a simple process known as bartering or trade, to put it in simple terms. A deed for a deed, a meal for a tool was a way of doing business. Although this might have sounded easier to provide, this didn't last long. Later the actual material of money in the form of coins, then on to paper was used to make business transactions.

I think money plays a huge part in everyone's life. Money can literally make or break you. It can position you high on the pedestal or deep down in the gutter. In some cases, the position money gives you may describe exactly who you are and what you deserve.

Like a man who built his business from the ground up may be seen and treated as a leader in his community, however sometimes money can make people misinterpret who a person really is. How hard working and deserving they truly are as well. For example, a boy or girl who was born into a rich, luxury-filled lifestyle while mooching off the earnings and hard work of those who came before them. Like how a prince is born into a position of wealth and power, a CEO's son/daughter is born an heir/heiress with a business they will one day run maybe for life.

I was raised with the best of both worlds. I was given wonderful financial blessings in my life. I was not raised blind to the values of money. All the responsible adults in my life instilled financial information in me. Over the years, I have use it and I will continue to use it in the future.

In a year from now I'll be applying to colleges. I will have a big decision to make at such a young age that will affect my whole life, but I'm not scared one bit. I'm not an encyclopedia on finances or anything, but I feel I am more educated on how money affects a person's life than the average teen, so I'm ready.

My plan is to graduate from high school one semester early and spend the remaining semester before going off to college working and saving my money. I want to enter as prepared as possible, especially financially. I am also going to apply for many scholarships. There are so many if you just take the time and look. Scholarships for having a high GPA, playing a sport, culinary experience and believe it or not, being left handed are just a few.

I have already established some career goals and set some plans for my future. Now all that's left is for me to put in the hard work and let God's plan fall into place!

I work a lot for the small things that I want and I understand that I will have to work for nearly everything I get in the future. However, that would be my reward to live a life where I was able to provide for myself and hopefully others.

NATAHLIA TUCKER

"Save Money and Money Will Save You"

I am 13 years old, in eighth grade living with my mother, father and my older sister, Nadia.

I feel money is a very silent thing. It's a very important part of everyone's lives. Some people can't get enough money, and others can't get money at all. A lot of people see money as a treasure reward for all the hard work they do, but to me the beauty isn't in making the money, it's in keeping it. From the day, I was eleven years old when I started digging in the bottom of my mom's purse looking for loose change for the ice cream truck, to thirteen years old, pulling out my teddy bear stash to help pay for my school lunch.

Between the time period of age eleven and thirteen, I learned that it is such a relief to know that I took the time to save my money for the times that I needed it the most. By growing up in a family with a successful background, I've learned I can make all the money I please, but if I don't think ahead, I would not know how beneficial this money could be for me.

When you were a little kid, do you remember a gift card for Christmas or your birthday? Remember you wanted to go to the toy store and your parents told you to spend your own money. Now fast forward one month later and you are sitting in the middle of the shopping mall with your friends and no one has any money. You're now wondering why you were so quick to spend that gift card instead of waiting for your parents to treat you.

It's because an investment in knowledge always pays the best interest. My example to explain this is that I still have most of my Christmas of 2013 money and it's now August of 2014. That's because I've learned that you must gain control of your money or the lack of it will forever control you.

If I can do it, you can too! I only receive money at yearly celebrations, not weekly paydays. You must think ahead and think smart when it comes to money. A wise person should have money in his or her head and not in the heart. Remember, "Save money and money will save you."

Summary

As you can see, our grandchildren are performing well. We are so very proud of all of them. The next step for all of them is to continue learning and practicing financial concepts and to expand into wealth building principles. It is never too early to start building a legacy of wealth.

Children do not ask to be brought into this world. As adults, parents, teachers, administrators, business leaders, members of the clergy, politicians and lawmakers, we all should do our best to educate and expose all children to this changing health and financial world. Get a home computer, or take them to the library. Get involved with the school they attend.

Meet the teachers, check the homework assignments, practice and discuss healthier eating and physical exercise. Give your child a hug and tell them you love them all the time. Sit down at the dinner table (with more fruits & vegetables) and talk to them about life goals and dreams. Meet the parents of their friends. Become an active member of your village, and help raise and educate all of our children.

To change the cycle of bad eating habits in our youth, one must take personal responsibility for eating healthier to achieve better wellness. Start by changing the eating and exercise habits for ourselves as well as our children. A lesson taught is a lessoned learned. That lesson might save your child from making some serious long term, hard to reverse bad financial habits in their future. Financial, as well as health and wellness education for our children go far beyond the classroom. Let's get back to that old school saying "It takes a village to raise a child."

REMEMBER "THE BEST IMPROVEMENT STARTS WITH SELF IMPROVEMENT."

POEM - "MONEY II"

Money means to me

Lots of responsibility

Bills, and checks, and things like that

Is not that easy to pay and that's a fact!

Money comes and disappears

When you reach for money your wallet is clear

You have to keep up with money, everywhere you go

Because when you see it's gone, it's a sad thing to know

Lots of responsibility

That is what money means to me!

-JANINA M. SPENCER

AT AGE 11

CHAPTER 10
LIVE WEALTHY-
LIVE HEALTHY

"Early to bed and early to rise
makes a man healthy, wealthy and wise."

-BENJAMIN FRANKLIN

W HAT IS MORE important? Being wealthy or being healthy? You don't have to choose. They are both equally important and obtainable with the right mindset, planning, and by taking informed action.

Below is a summary of our 7 LIVE W.E.A.L.T.H.Y. PRINCIPLES that we live by. They are the cornerstone that formed the company's financial education and coaching wings.

We introduced our 7 LIVE W.E.A.L.T.H.Y. PRINCIPLES, for the first time to the world, live on stage in front of over +1,200 attendees from 20+ countries, in Johannesburg, South Africa at the JT Foxx Tycoons of Wealth event. We also shared the stage with Nelson Mandela's grandson, Ndaba Mandela and fellow South African- multiple Olympic Medalist-Wayde van

Niekerk and Randi Zuckerberg-Former Director of Facebook Marketing.

7 LIVE W.E.A.L.T.H.Y. PRINCIPLES

Our 7 Live W.E.A.L.T.H.Y. Principles is a proven system for financial transformational change and success. They will help you change the way to Think, Act and Feel about your money.

Zig Ziglar said: "Money isn't the most important thing in life, but it's reasonably close to oxygen on the 'gotta have it' scale."

Each of the letters in the word W.E.A.L.T.H.Y. represent a principle. If you apply these principles to your daily life, you will be able to "transform your Financial DNA for Life". Obtain the level of financial security and freedom you desire. But it requires action on your part. Financial security and freedom is not a get rich, abracadabra wave the magic wand process. It takes commitment, focus, time and education to reach your financial goals.

THE 1ST PRINCIPLE IS W FOR WEALTH MINDSET

First thing's first, you must change the way you think about your money, act with your money, and feel about your money. You must think like the wealthy so that you can move in that direction and get rid of old school broke mentally paradigms.

THE 2ND PRINCIPLE IS E FOR ENTREPRENEURSHIP

You can't get wealthy working a 9 to 5 job. The math just doesn't work. If you work 40 hours a week for 40 years, you get to retire with 40% of your income. If you can't live off of $100,000 a year today, what makes you think you can live your current lifestyle off of $40,000?

THE 3RD PRINCIPLE IS A FOR ASSET MANAGEMENT

What is your biggest asset? Many of you may have answered your "home." Well, unless your home is paid in full and providing you a source of income, I hate to break it to you, but your home is not an asset. Money is constantly being paid out monthly for 15 to 30 years in most cases even after the home is paid off. So, if you pay a mortgage, gas, light, lawn care service or snow removal, and house repairs, it is a liability.

THE 4TH PRINCIPLE IS L FOR LEAVE A LEGACY

Webster's dictionary defines legacy as: "something transmitted by or received from an ancestor or predecessor or from the past." But legacy is not just about the material things you leave for someone. It is what you leave in them that will allow them to survive, thrive and pass it forward.

Legacy/Estate Planning

According to a 2015 Rocket Lawyer survey, 64% of Americans do not have a will. The number is higher for younger Americans, 70% for those 45-54 and 55% for those 55+. People put off creating and estate plan because they don't want to deal with their own death or incapacitation. But it is necessary to ensure your hard earn assets, as well as your children are left in the care of the people that you want.

THE 5TH PRINCIPLE IS T FOR TITHING AND PHILANTHROPY

"To whom much is given, to him much is expected."

This quote has ancient biblical origins; however, today's meaning can be translated as being "socially conscience". We are all connected globally and should give back to our local and global community.

The Merriam-Webster dictionary defines tithing as: "a tenth part of something paid as a voluntary contribution, or as a tax especially for the support of a religious establishment."

Typically, tithing is the way some faithful give back to their local religious group. It's up to the religious leaders to decide how the funds are used. However, the concept of tithing may or may not be applicable to all religious groups.

Philanthropy, according to the dictionary, is "goodwill to fellow members of the human race; *especially*: active effort to promote human welfare."

THE 6TH PRINCIPLE IS H FOR HEALTHY LIVING

As stated above both your wealth and your health are equally important.

Adopt healthy living habits so you can live long wealthy life. Most of what I am going to share with you is just common sense that we already know. But sometimes it helps to hear it to get us motivated to make the necessary changes.

Start by controlling what you put in your mouth. Next, the most important thing is to visit the doctor and dentist, at least once a year to help detect and prevent diseases early. Get yearly mammograms, prostate checks, a cardio stress test/work-up, chest x-rays, blood and urine tests. These basic tests can save your life by finding issues early.

THE 7TH PRINCIPLE IS Y FOR YOU ARE IN CONTROL

Question: Have you ever thought about where the biggest room in the world is located?

Answer: The biggest room in the world is the room for improvement!

Discover your "WHY." Define your goals and dreams, your reason and purpose. You may be too focused on daily living. You must allow your future to drive your daily living and get your head and your heart in-sync.

You must make a conscious DECISION to control your life! Visit us at www.tmeginc.com to learn more about our 7 LIVE W.E.A.L.T.H.Y. Principles, our workshops, coaching programs and speaking engagements.

Also, check out our health products so you can Live Wealthy and Live Healthy-You Gotta Do Both!

Remember, the Best Improvement Starts with Self-Improvement!

CHAPTER 11
START YOUR SELF-IMPROVEMENT

*"You don`t have to be great to get started, but
you have to get started to be great."*

-LES BROWN

I TRY TO IMPROVE myself on an ongoing daily basis. Instead
of making excuses I attempt to get a full understanding
by doing my own due diligence and research. If I do not
understand something, I am not afraid to ask someone who
is in a position to give me the answer. I respect others feeling
and thoughts even if I disagree. For me, learning is a life-long
process that begins at birth and ends at death.

Now that you have read this book, here is a chance for you
to evaluate some of your past and present thoughts about how
you think, act and feel about money. If you are single, you
have sole responsibility for yourself. If you are married, you
each have the responsibility and accountability. If you need to
change some things in your life, maybe you can start by first
changing your thoughts about your situation. Evaluate your
past actions to determine what you did wrong so you DON'T

make the same mistakes going forward. Do not dwell on the past, look to the future by changing the present.

Procrastination has been and continues to be the assassin of success. How often do you say "I wish I could do this or that, or have this or that"? Are you a wanna doer, a gonna doer or a never doer?

Do you have a fear of success with the word FEAR meaning False Evidence Appearing Real? Are you the person who is holding you back from your personal success? You might ask yourself, how do I get started? Am I willing to step out of my comfort zone? What will my plan of action be? "Can I really get out debt? Can I improve my credit? Can I start saving, and then eventually investing? Can I transform my Financial DNA For Life?

The answer is YES to every single question above. It first starts with the belief that you can do it. Next your burning desire must be laser focused toward accomplishment. Then you must have FAITH and take ACTION. One without the other will not get the job done.

That's it, that's all. There are no magic trick words like Abracadabra or Hocus Pocus. There is no hand clapping illusion trick that will cause your financial situation to change. That is all smoke and mirrors and never will contribute to your overall troubles disappearing. By now you know what it will take for you to move forward.

Do not be a victim of procrastination. Below are 12 steps you can take right away to begin the process of changing your financial situation:

12 STEPS TO FINANCIAL CHANGE

1. Make a personal commitment to yourself to change your financial situation. Write down a list of your short-term, medium, and long-term financial goals clearly defined with dates of accomplishments. Sign it and have it witnessed and use it as a tool to hold yourself accountable!
2. Start a spending plan and track your expenses and stick to it.
3. Reduce your expenses – Review Chapter 1 – Step 5A.

4. Start the Debt Elimination Rollover Payment Plan – Review Chapter 1 - Step 5B.

5. Cut up your credit cards if you have out of control spending. Negotiate a lower interest rate, or transfer current high balances to a lower or zero percent interest rate card. Pay more than the minimum due, pay your bills on time.

6. Create your income and expense statement and calculate your net worth – Review Chapter 3.

7. Open an interest-bearing savings account and start saving (minimum whatever you can afford, but do it regularly). Consider the 52-Week Saving Plan in Chapter 4. Next, self-educate and learn how to invest.

8. Obtain your free credit report and repair any inaccurate information.

9. Create a six-month to a nine-month emergency savings account that will cover your total monthly expenses. Expect the unexpected. Be Prepared.

10. Be patient and don't quit. Follow your action plan.

11. Learn more about transforming your Financial DNA For Life at www.tmeginc.com.

12. Last but not least, and equally important, find a way to be of service. Consider giving back through volunteering your time, product, or financial resources to a cause you are passionate about. If you can't find one, create one!

There are also some things you can do right now to begin to improve yourself through education:

- Visit our website at (www.tmeginc.com) and view our products and services.
- Get a library card and use it. You can check out financial literacy educational materials for free and also block out computer time if you don't own one.
- Read financial magazines, the financial section of the newspapers, financial books and tapes in a quiet environment.

- Learn the basic use of a computer and how to use the internet for research.
- Make learning through continuing education a lifelong process.

I think by now you get the point. If you need to make some changes in your life, by all means, make some changes in your life. Success is different for everyone. What measure of success will determine your happiness? What are you willing to do to obtain your actual success? When you grow old and you look back at life, are you going to ask yourself, "If I could have, If would have, I should have, but I did not?" Or are you willing to do today what others won't, so tomorrow you can live like others don't?

We all have choices to make in life. We must not be hindered by negative thinking. Take action now toward obtaining your goals and dreams. Develop a sound plan that will guide you up the ladder of success. Be determined to overcome the fear of failure, and the laughter and other negative things you might encounter along the way toward achievement. It has been said that "The sky is the limit", but I like the saying, "If you reach for the moon, you will touch some shining stars along the way."

First you think it, and when you start to believe it, take action toward it, only then can you achieve it. Next, your willingness to believe in yourself, your idea, and your plan is critical to your success. You must have a never, ever, give up or quit attitude. With these tools, attitudes and behaviors, you can experience the sweet taste of long-lasting success that you have been searching for.

Step out of your comfort zone and don't let FEAR, uncertainty or lack of knowledge hold you back from whatever it is that you want to accomplish in life. You must seize the moment of opportunity and that moment is NOW! **REMEMBER,"THE BEST IMPROVEMENT STARTS WITH SELF IMPROVEMENT"**

PERSONAL CHECK LIST
FOR CHANGE

What ideas did you read that were of significant value to you? Below list the steps you will take immediately to improve your overall personal financial situation that will help lead you down the road to success. You must define what success means to you, what you want to accomplish and most importantly when you want to achieve it!

1. _____

2. _____

3. _____

4. _____

5. _____

6. _____

7. _____

8. _____

9. _____

10. _____

I will take charge of my/our personal finances, health and wellness because I/we believe that "The Best Improvement Starts With Self Improvement." I/we will not allow procrastination to become the assassination of my/our success! I/we will get started TODAY.

My Signature _____

Date _____

"THE BEST IMPROVEMENT
STARTS WITH SELF IMPROVEMENT"

CONCLUSION

"There`s only one way to succeed in anything,
and that is to give it everything."

-VINCENT LOMBARDI

D R. MARTIN LUTHER King Jr. gave a historic speech in Washington D.C., concerning equal rights for all people. He stressed that regardless of your race, color, or creed you are entitled to have the opportunity to pursue and live the dream of your undertaking. King also emphasized the importance of economic freedom as one of his many platforms for change.

There are universal laws that apply to everyone, such as the Law of Cause and Effect. The cause of being prepared for an opportunity can increase the effect of it actually occurring. Meaning, the financial literacy lifelong educational journey will cause you to change many things in your life. The effect of that change will not only impact your life, it will also affect the lives of many for generations that follow behind!

When you succeed, you spend more money, which helps stimulate the economy in your community. When you purchase goods and services, the trickle-down economic law of cause and effects kicks into gear. Starting with the manufacturer, supplier of the transportation, import/export dock workers, merchants owners, employees and government taxes, everyone can benefit or make a profit because YOU spent some of your wealth!

It is believed that there are three classes of people in America: the upper class, the middle class, and the lower class. Is it possible for a person who is considered to be in the lower class to advance to the ranks of the middle and upper classes? Yes, it is, because what all three classes have in common is the ability to learn more from a formal college or university education and/or a self-help education. Either can lead to more opportunities to earn more for all who actively seek wisdom.

There are many improvements and new additions in this world that came from one single thought or idea from someone who developed singleness of purpose to fulfill their desired objective in life.

The income gap between every level from down on Main Street, all the way up to Wall Street and beyond may never be equal. But wouldn't it be nice to reach the millionaire or billionaire level. This level could afford you the opportunity to help your family, friends, and strangers who are in need of a hand up, not hand out! Or just be able to live financially secure without relying on government assistance.

With wealth, social consciousness should follow with some degree of responsibility for uplifting the community using some of your resources to help others. Providing employment, affordable housing, training and assistance or whatever service you want to champion, by all means you will be able to do it.

Have you considered what led the wealthy to their success and what is stopping you from obtaining yours? Ordinary people can accomplish extraordinary things. With a big dream, followed by a plan of action, persistence, and a burning desire to become successful, the way will present itself! Their success was achieved because they had a definite purpose in life and a willingness to succeed at all cost, against all odds. They did not allow stumbling blocks, roadblocks, or negative people to hold them back. Instead, they forged on until victory was achieved.

Don't continue blindly following the masses down the 40-40-40 earned income path. Working 40 hours per week, working 40 long years of your life, so you can retire and live on 40% of your income! Stop just working hard for your money and exchanging hours for dollars! Start walking down the passive income path and learn how to create and build wealth by making your money start working for you!

And for the millennials, avoid the mistakes of taking out too much student loan debt, not saving, not investing in your companies 401k as soon as you become eligible and buying things on credit just to keep up with the Joneses or the reality TV stars!

No matter what your status in life is to date, having a dream, developing a plan of action for self-achievement, setting goals, and having a positive mental attitude can assist you in your quest for success. You might stand alone in your beliefs, but in the darkest hours you can always depend on your inner self as long as you believe, then you can achieve!

Success is different for all people, but none the less, success at one time or another has been thought about by everyone, but only sought after by some! Re-read this book and please keep an open mind and focus in on your situation and what you can do to improve it. If you think you can, you can. If you think you can't, you can't. Either way you are right! Take action today!

REMEMBER, "THE BEST IMPROVEMENT STARTS WITH SELF IMPROVEMENT"

POEM - REAL HARD LOOK

Now that you read this book

Step back, and take a real hard look

Is your money low, and your debt high

Did your misjudgments cause, a tear in your eye

Is your credit bad, from spending all you had

Are you doing just fine, and feeling real glad

Should you make some changes, to stay on track

Your once good credit, you can build it back

No more excuses, that's enough you see

Because self-improvement will help, set you free!

-MICHAEL" BART" MATHEWS

DISCLAIMER

I AM NOT A certified financial planner, licensed public accountant, attorney or real estate agent. I do not practice in the medical profession. I am not a credit counselor or a debt consolidation specialist by trade. I am not a licensed Pastor, but I do have an unwavering amount of spirituality, filled with faith and belief in the creator and the universe. I am not offering financial or medical advice. I am providing examples of my negative adversities and positives changes by using financial literacy education. I highly recommend you consult a professional in any area outlined in this book before you take action.

While every attempt has been made to provide accurate information, I am not accountable for any errors or omissions. Many of the examples have come from my personal experiences and from internet research using reputable websites.

Some things in my past have been outlined in detail to inform you of the low points that I also had to overcome. I do not promise any kind of future results in your life based on this book. Because my financial life has unbelievably, positively changed beyond any expectations, I shared with you several plans of action that have worked for me.

I take full responsibility for my past actions and hold no one person accountable. I have accepted my past as I move on to the future by changing my life in the present. I understand that learning is a lifelong process and some do, some don't, some will and some won't! Learning is here for all who seeks her wisdom and favor!

GLOSSARY

Adjustable Rate Mortgage (ARM)
A mortgage that allows periodic adjustments of the interest rate, based on changes in a specific index.

Affordable Health Care Act (ACA)
A government mandate that forces health insurance companies to play by the rules prohibiting them from discriminating against anyone with a pre-existing condition, dropping your coverage if you get sick, billing you into bankruptcy because of an illness or injury, and limiting your annual or lifetime benefits. You won't need to worry about losing coverage if you get laid off or change jobs. Also, insurance companies are required to cover your preventive care screenings.

Amortization
A mathematical calculation used to estimate the reduction of debt from monthly loan repayments. It also determines how much of your repayment goes towards the principal and how much goes toward the interest.

Annual Percentage Rate
The annual rate that is charged for borrowing (or earned on savings), expressed as a single percentage number that represents the actual yearly cost of funds over the term of a loan. This includes any fees or additional costs associated with the transaction.

Annuity

A contractual financial product sold by financial institutions that are designed to accept and grow funds that are paid out at a later point in time. They are usually used to provide fixed income during retirement.

Appraisal

The gathering of information on the same type of properties in the form of a written report that reflects the value of the property as is or in repaired condition.

Asset

A resource having economic value that an individual, corporation or country owns or controls with the expectation that it will provide future benefits.

Available Balance

The balance in checking, savings and other types of financial accounts that the account holder can spend, withdraw or transfer. If a check deposit has not been cleared by the issuing bank, the funds will not be available to the account holder even though they may show up in the account's stated total funds. The net effect is that the account available balance may be different from the ledger balance.

Average Daily Balance

Calculated by summing an account's daily ending balances within the billing cycle and then divide by the number of days in the billing cycle.

Bankruptcy

The state of a person or firm unable to repay debts and being legally relieved of the debt obligation by the court.

Balance Sheet

A list of your assets and liabilities outlining your net worth.

Bear Market

Low stock market conditions indicating prices of securities are falling or expecting to fall.

Beneficiary

A person or persons listed on an insurance policy, trust, financial account as the designated receiver of benefits upon the death of the document owner.

Benign

A growth on or within the body that is not cancerous.

Better Business Bureau (BBB)

An organization which promotes accountability, reliability, and creditability in business across the U. S. by providing business ratings, dispute resolution services, consumer education and alerts.

Bonds

A financial investment in which the investor loans money to an entity (company or government) that borrows the funds for a defined period of time at a specified interest rate.

Broker

1. An individual or firm that charges a fee or commission for executing buy and sell orders submitted by investors.
2. The role of a firm when it acts as an agent for a customer and charges the customer a commission for its services.
3. A licensed real estate professional who typically represents the seller of a property.

Bull Market

A high stock market condition which prices for securities are rising or expected to rise.

Capitalism

An economic and political system characterized by a free market enterprise in which a country's trade and industry are controlled by private owners for profit, rather than by the state.

Capital Gain

The profit from the sale of a property or investment that results when the sale price is higher than the initial purchase price.

Capital Loss

The absence of a profit from the sale of a property or investment that results when the sale price is lower than the initial purchase price.

Certificate of Deposit (CD)

A type of savings instrument entitling bearer to receive interest upon maturity. A CD bears a maturity date. Interest can be calculated daily, monthly, quarterly, etc.

Compounding

The effect of calculated interest when added to the principal so that the interest itself also earns interest.

Dividend Re-Investment Plan (DRIP)

A plan offered by a corporation allowing investors to reinvest their cash dividends by purchasing additional shares or fractional shares on the dividend payment date.

Debt/Liability

Any amount of money borrowed and owed by one party to another.

Default

The failure to promptly pay interest or principal when due.

Diversification

A risk management technique that mixes a wide variety of investments within a portfolio.

Dollar Cost Averaging

The technique of buying a fixed dollar amount of a particular investment on a regular schedule regardless of the share price. More shares are purchased when the price is low, and fewer shares are purchased when the price is higher.

Earnings Per Share (EPS)

The profit remaining on a per share basis that a company has available to pay dividends or reinvest in itself.

Entrepreneur

An individual who, rather than working as an employee, owns and operates a small business and assumes all the risk and reward of a given business venture, idea, or goods or service offered for sale.

Estate

All of the things an individual owns such as real estate, art collections, collectibles, antiques, jewelry, investments, life insurance, etc. that have value to them.

Equity
1. The difference between the current market value of the property and the amount the owner owes on the property.
2. The value of shares issued by a company.

Fair Isaac Credit Organization (FICO) Score
A standard numbering system ranging from 300-850 contained within your credit report that credit bureaus sell to lenders so they can assess an applicant's credit risk and whether to issue or extend credit.

Federal Deposit Insurance Corporation (FDIC)
The entity that insures your deposits up to $250,000 in case an FDIC-insured banking institution fails. The insurance covers checking, savings and money market accounts, and certificates of deposit, or CDs. It also includes other types of accounts, such as individual retirement accounts, or IRAs, and trust accounts. Also, each owner of a joint account is insured up to the limit. Also, each of their single owned accounts is insured as well.

Federal Insurance Contributions Act (FICA)
A law in the U. S. requiring a deduction from paychecks and income that goes toward the Social Security program and Medicare. Both employees and employers are responsible for sharing the FICA payments.

Foreclosure
A legal procedure when property used as security for a debt is sold to satisfy the debt when the present owner fails to make payments.

Home Equity Line of Credit (HELOC)
A line of credit is extended to a homeowner that uses the borrower's home as collateral. The borrower may draw down on the loan at his or her discretion. Interest is charged at a predetermined interest rate usually based on prevailing prime rates.

Home Equity Loan
A loan based on the equity that the owner has in the property.

Income and Expense Statement

A financial statement that provides a summary of income and expenses/debts incurred by an individual or business to assess their performance over a specific period of time.

Interest Rate

1. The effective rate charged on borrowed money.
2. The effective rate paid on savings or investments.

Interest

1. The dollar amount charged for the privilege of borrowing money (APR).
2. The amount of ownership a stockholder has in a company (percentage).
3. The dollar amount earned on an investment.

Insurance

A contract purchased to guarantee compensation for a specified loss.

Insured Peril

A specific source of loss for which a policy will provide protection such as lightning, fire, smoke, explosion, riot, vandalism, hail, and theft.

IRA-Individual Retirement Account

1. **Traditional IRA** is a retirement plan account under U.S. law designed to allow an individual to save for retirement. Funds are eligible for withdrawal after age 59 ½. Contributions can be made before-tax or after-tax. Any after-tax contributions and earnings are taxable as earned income upon withdrawal. However, funds can be withdrawn prior to 59 ½ but an additional 10% income tax penalty will be assessed.
2. **Roth IRA** is a retirement plan account under U.S. law designed to allow an individual to save for retirement. Only after-tax contributions can be made. All contributions and earnings withdrawn after 5 years and after reaching age 59 ½ are tax-free and penalty-free for life. However, funds can be withdrawn outside of these rules and will incur taxes and an additional 10% penalty.
3. **401k/457** are employer-sponsored retirement plan accounts under U.S. law designed to allow an individual

to save for retirement. The withdrawal rules are generally the same as a Traditional IRA. Some employers will match a percentage of the employee contribution.

Judgement

A legal ruling in favor of one party but against the other party in a lawsuit.

Ledger Balance

The balance of a customer account as shown on the bank statement. The ledger balance is found by subtracting the total number of debits from the total number of credits for a given accounting period. The ledger balance is used solely in the reconciliation of book balances.

Lien

The claim of a creditor against property.

Malignant

A growth on or within the body that is cancerous.

Medicaid

A government program that provides medical assistance for persons with low income.

Medicare

A federal health insurance plan for people who have reached full retirement age and for those who are receiving Social Security disability benefits may also qualify.

Mortgage

A loan to finance the purchase of real estate usually with specified payment periods of time and interest rates.

Mutual Funds

A collections of securities that gives the investors access to a well-diversified portfolio of equities, bonds, and other securities. Each shareholder may participate in the gain or loss of the fund.

National Association of Investment Clubs (NAIC)

An organization which provides investment education and resources.

Nest Egg

A sum of money saved or invested for a specific future purpose, usually retirement.

Periodic Interest Rate

The interest rate charged on a loan or realized on an investment over a given period of time. Most interest rates are quoted on an annual basis. This rate is calculated by dividing the annual interest rate (APR) by the number of compounding periods.

Philanthropy

The desire to promote the welfare of others expressed primarily by the generous donation of money to good causes.

Probate

The legal process (court proceedings) of administering the estate of a deceased person. This is necessary to resolve all claims and distribute the deceased's personal property via a will or in the absence of a will.

Portfolio

A group of assets such as stocks, bonds, mutual funds, real estate and cash held by an investor.

Price to Earnings (PE) Ratio

An equity valuation multiple of a company's current share price compared to its per-share earnings. Calculated by dividing the company's Market Value per Share by Earnings per Share (EPS).

Prime Rate

It is an interest rate determined by individual banks. It is often used as a reference rate (also called the base rate) for many types of loans, including loans to small businesses, home equity loans, and credit card loans. It is based on the federal funds rate, which is set by the Federal Reserve.

Principal

1. The face value of a bond.
2. The amount borrowed or the amount still owed on a loan.
3. The original amount invested separately from earnings.

Private Equity

An asset class consisting of equity securities and debt that is not publicly traded on a stock exchange. Private equity is a source of investment capital from high net worth individuals or companies. Private equity firms, angel investors and venture capital firms make investments directly into a private company for the purpose of earning a profit and acquiring equity ownership in that company.

Reverse Mortgage

A special type of government insured loan used to convert the equity in a home into cash. The money obtained in a reverse mortgage is usually used to provide seniors with financial security in their retirement years. (Special qualifying rules may apply for acceptance not limited to the following: age of applicant, proof of home ownership and condition of home based on inspection results).

Rule of 72

A method to find the number of years required to double your money at a given interest rate. You divide the interest rate by 72. Example if you expect to receive a 6% interest rate, you divide 72 by 6 which equals 12 years for the principal amount to double using the magic of compound interest reinvested.

Social Security Income (SSI)

Government income for people who have reached retirement age and/or for people who have become disabled or has a disability approved by a licensed medical doctor.

Social Security Statement- SSA-7005

A report containing your social security benefits calculated estimates based on your work history giving you a snapshot of your SSA contributions as well as your potential earnings. Can be mailed or accessed online via the SSA website by workers starting at age 25.

Stocks

A type of security giving ownership in a corporation and represents a claim on part of the corporation's assets and earnings. Stocks are also known as shares or equity.

Stock Selection Guide (SSG)

It is a paper form (tool) developed by the NAIC in 1950 to assist individual investors in the fundamental analysis and selection of growth stocks. It helps to determine the relative value of a stock which are most likely to increase in the next 5 years. It also requires the investor to apply his or her own judgment to many of the factors during the analysis process.

Trust

A fiduciary relationship in which one party known as a trustor, gives another party the trustee, the right to hold title to property or assets for the benefit of the trustor and/or a third party, the beneficiary. Here are 4 primary categories of trusts:

1. Living Trust – a trust that is in effect during the trustor's lifetime
2. Testamentary Trust – a trust that is created through the will of a deceased person
3. Land Trust – a trust that is created to hold/record real estate and protect the identity of the beneficial owner
4. Insurance Trust – an irrevocable, non-amendable trust which is both the owner and beneficiary of one or more insurance policies. Used to set aside cash proceeds upon death as life insurance is currently exempt from the taxable estate of the decedent.

Umbrella Liability Insurance

A type of insurance designed to provide added liability protection above and beyond the limits on homeowners, auto, and watercraft personal policies. This protection is intended to kick-in when the liability amount on other current policies has been exhausted.

Will

A legally enforceable declaration of how a person wishes his or her property to be distributed after death. A will may be required to go through a Probate (court) process before it can be fully executed.

APPENDIX-RESOURCES

Below is a list of resources in support of and for additional information on the various organizations and topics throughout this book. The links and other contact information provided below were valid at the time this book went to market. There is no guarantee they will continue to be valid. Searching the internet is the best way to find current information on any subject within this book.

Affordable Health Care Act (ACA): online sign up
Health Insurance Market Place
Department of Health and Human Services
465 Industrial Blvd.
London Kentucky, 40750-0001
www.healthcare.gov

Health Care Help Line Numbers (enrollment assistance via telephone)
Or request your paper application to be mailed to you.
(800) 318-2596
(855) 889-4325 - TTY

American Heart Association
www.heart.org/HEARTORG

National Association of Attorney Generals-Find your State`s Attorney General
   www.naag.org

Better Business Bureau: search the BBB directory for your city and state
   www.bbb.org

Cancer: research and prevention
   American Cancer Society
   www.americancancersociety.com

   (800) 227-2345
   www.preventioncancer.org

   Susan G. Komen Breast Cancer Organization
   ww5.komen.org

City Colleges of Chicago: Star Scholarship-Tuition Free Program Info
   (773) 265-5343 (COLLEGE)
   www.ccc.edu
   starscholarship@ccc.edu

College Planning: research
   www.collegeboard.com
   www.finaid.org
   www.savingforcollege.com
   www.tiaa-cref.org/public/products-services/
   education-savings

National Foundation For Consumer Credit Counseling Services
   (800) 388-2227

Consumer Credit Protection Act: Laws Protecting Consumer Rights
   America`s Debt Help
   www.debt.org/credit/your-consumer-rights/protection-act

Federal Deposit Insurance Corporation www.fdic.gov/regulations/laws/rules/6500-100.html

Federal Trade Commission
www.ftc.gov/ogc/stat3.shtm

Consumer Financial Protection Bureau
www.ftc.gov/bcp/about.shtm

Consumer Federal Trade Commission (FTC) – Bureau of Consumer Protection
www.consumer.ftc.gov

Consumer Credit Reporting Agency (Bureau): For disputing or correcting information in your credit file contact the company that provided you with the credit report first. Also, VantageScore resource.
Equifax
(800) 685-1111
www.equifax.com

Equifax Fraud Assistance Service
(800) 525-6285

Experian
(888) 397-3742
www.experian.com

Trans Union
(877) 322-8228
www.transunion.com

Trans Union Fraud Victim Assistance Department (FVAD)
(800) 680-7289

Credit Card: information sources
Bankrate: www.bankrate.com
CardRating: www.cardratings.com
CardWeb: www.cardweb.com

Credit Report: free annual credit report
Annual Credit Report Request Service
P.O. Box 105281
Atlanta, GA 30348-5281
(877) 322-8228
www.annualcreditreport.com

Credit Prescreen/Opt-Out
P.O. Box 600344
Jacksonville, FL 32260
(888) 567-8688
www.OptOutPrescreen.com

Credit Report/Score Monitoring: some provide free services
www.credit.com
www.creditkarma.com
your.vantagescore.com

Diabetes
www.americandiabetesassociation.com

Dow Jones Industrial Historical Averages: Wall Street Journal
quotes.wsj.com/DJIA/index-historical-prices

Employee Benefits Security Administration, United States Department of Labor:
(866)-444-3272
www.dol.gov/ebsa

Fair Credit Reporting Act (FCRA)
www.ftc.gov/os/statutes/fcrajump.shtm

Fair Isaac Corporation (FICO): credit score information
www.myfico.com

Federal Deposit Insurance Corporation (FDIC)
(877) 275-3342
www.fdic.gov

Financial Literacy Education Source
www.financiallit.org
www.investopedia.com

Financial Planner and Advisors: locating sources
American Institute of CPA`s
www.aicpa.org

Certified Financial Planner Board of Standards
www.cfp-board.org

Financial Planning Association (FPA)
(800) 322-4237
www.fpanet.org

National Association of Personal Financial Advisors
(NAPFA)
(888) 333-6659
www.napfa.org

Society of Financial Service Professionals
www.financialpro.org

Foreclosure Information Sources and Assistance
Making Homes Affordable
www.makinghomeaffordable.gov/Pages/default.aspx

Home Owners Preserving Equity (HOPE) National
www.hopenow.com
(888)-995-HOPE (4673)

(HUD) U.S. Department of Housing and Urban
Development
www.hud.gov/foreclosure

Identity Theft: information and reporting
Federal Trade Commission (FTC)
(877) 438-4338
www.identitytheft.gov
www.ftc.gov/idtheft

Insurance Company's Rating Sources
A.M. Best Company
(908)-439-2200
www.ambest.com

Moody`s
(212) 553-1653
www.moodys.com

Kids and Money: sources
www.kids.usa.gov
www.kidsmoney.org

Let`s Move! Initiative, First Lady Michelle Obama
www.letsmove.gov
www.letsmoveschools.org

Mortgage: rates, calculators, and information sources –
there are numerous sources for rates and information on the
internet. Here is a couple to get you started:
www.bankrates.com
www.hsh.com

Mutual Funds – research
www.mfea.com
www.morningstar.com

National Association of Investor Corp – (NAIC): investment
club information
www.better-investing.org

National Council on Aging
www.ncoa.org

National Stroke Association
  www.stroke.org

Organization for Economic Co-operation and Development (OECD)
  www.oecd.org

President's Council on Fitness
  www.fitness.gov

Reverse Mortgage
  Federal Trade Commission-Reverse Mortgage Information
  www.consumer.ftc.gov/articles/0192-reverse-mortgages

  HUD Reverse Mortgage Portal
  portal.hud.gov

  HUD Reverse Mortgage Counselor Search
  entp.hud.gov/idapp/html/hecm_agency_look.cfm

  National Reverse Mortgage Lenders Association
  www.reversemortgage.org

Social Security Administration
  (800) 772-1213
  www.socialsecurity.gov

Social Security Fraud Hotline
  (800) 269-0271

U.S. Department of Education-Federal Student Aid
Student Loan Repayment Information
  www.studentaid.ed.gov/sa/repay-loans

United States Treasury
  www.treasury.gov

ABOUT THE AUTHOR

MICHAEL "BART" MATHEWS is a successful published Author, Entrepreneur, Real Estate Investor, Motivational Speaker and Certified Professional Life Coach. He is the co-founder of The Mathews Entrepreneur Group, Inc (TMEG). He is dedicated and committed to providing a Personal Financial Literacy Education Program and one-on-one financial literacy mentoring via books and workshops along with an online educational platform. He will also publish entertaining and exciting books for pleasure reading in different literary genres.

Michael spent 30 years in the private and public Transportation industry where he held various management and bus operator/line instructor roles. He retired from the Chicago Transit Authority in 2012.

Early in his career, Michael experienced financial setbacks which motivated him to learn how to take control of his personal finances. He was inspired to write his first book to share, with others, his newfound knowledge on how to improve your personal finances.

Michael also served as the assistant treasurer of the "Blessed to Invest" Investment Club furthering his personal financial literacy educational journey.

The first edition of his book titled Financially Speaking: The Best Improvement Starts with Self-Improvement was self-published in 2008, the second edition was also self-published in 2015. As an author, Michael`s love and passion for writing has led him to write both fiction and non-fiction books for the ultimate purpose of "Educating and Entertaining the Planet!"

Michael was born and raised on the south side of Chicago Illinois. As a young adult, he attended Bray Temple CME Church where his spiritual guidance was nurtured. He was educated in the Chicago Public School System graduating from Paul Revere Grammar School and Hirsch High School.

While attending Hirsch High School, Michael was a member of the 1973 Boys Class AA Chicago City Basketball Championship team. They went on to the win the Illinois Class AA State Championship as well. Also, the entire Hirsch basketball team along with their coach were inducted into the Illinois High School Association (IHSA) Hall of Fame in 1993. They were also inducted into the Chicago Public League Basketball Coaches Association (CPLBCA) Hall of Fame in 2013.

Michael did his undergraduate studies at Lincoln University in Jefferson City, Missouri, and the University of Wisconsin-Parkside in Kenosha, Wisconsin, where he played basketball at both universities.

Michael also played basketball in the European League based in Salzburg Austria. Michael has traveled throughout the United States as well as to numerous countries throughout Europe.

Michael`s burning desire and heartfelt mission is to give back to society. During his employment with the Chicago Transit Authority, he regularly donated to the (HBCU) Historically Black College and University Scholarship Fund to help grow our future leaders. Michael continues his mission to give back to the community by investing in companies that have established charitable platforms for giving back. Michael is committed to his personal pledge of donating a portion of the proceeds from his book sales to causes dear to his heart. He wants to uplift the lives of men, women and children by giving them a hand-up and not a handout while they are in a transitional period in life!

With your purchase of this book, along with your continued support of Michael's other upcoming projects, you will be giving back as well. Remember, "Teamwork, makes the Dreamwork."

Michael is working on several other manuscripts scheduled for completion and publication in 2016.

Michael is married to Robbie, both attended the Certified Life Coach Institute of Orange County, and successfully graduated becoming Certified Professional Life Coaches. The Certified Life Coach Institute of Orange County is approved by the International Coaching Federation (ICF) and is also a member of the Association of Coach Training Organizations (ACTO).

Michael and Robbie reside in Illinois and enjoy traveling and spending time with their grandchildren.

Visit his website at www.tmeginc.com to join his mailing list.

Thank you in advance for your support!

REMEMBER "THE BEST IMPROVEMENT STARTS WITH SELF IMPROVEMENT"

FINANCIALLY SPEAKING
THE BEST IMPROVEMENT STARTS WITH SELF IMPROVEMENT
Create Your Own Economic Stimulus Plan
Second Edition

By
Michael "Bart" Mathews

To place your online orders, visit our secure website
www.tmeginc.com

Or

To Order by Mail – send cashier's check or money
order to
The Mathews Entrepreneur Group, Inc.
1020 Park Drive Suite 491
Flossmoor IL, 60422-1711

Or

Email: info@tmeginc.com

Or

Call 1-800-369-TMEG (8634)

You can download all of the worksheets in this book at
www.tmeginc.com

Google "Michael Bart Mathews" to locate him via the
internet.

Michael is available to conduct book signings,
speaking engagements, panel discussions and financial
literacy workshops at schools, churches, corporations,
social and business associations, book clubs, and other
community organizations!

Printed in the United States
By Bookmasters